Big Fish
to
Rubber Ducky

IAN BRADLEY

Copyright © 2015 Ian Bradley

All rights reserved.

ISBN: 0994355505

ISBN-13: 978-0-9943555-0-8

DEDICATION

For Kate, who was there but too young to remember...

CONTENTS

Acknowledgements

1 *It Wasn't My Fault…*	p.1
2 *"Seguimos Adelante."*	p.14
3 *Is it a House or is it a Boat?*	p.19
4 *The Best Laid Plans.*	p.32
5 *A Place with a View.*	p.42
6 *Something for Posterity.*	p.51
7 *This is Our House!*	p.57
8 *Walking on Water.*	p.65
9 *Scotch and Water Don't Mix.*	p.73
10 *The Race is On.*	p.81
11 *Scotch on the Rocks.*	p.89
12 *"The Compleat Angler."*	p.98

CONTENTS (cont.)

13 *It's Only a Game.*   *p.105*

14 *Round One…*   *p.115*

15 *No More Races!*   *p.122*

16 *Back to the Land.*   *p.130*

17 *A Prickly Point.*   *p.137*

18 *Round Two…*   *p.146*

19 *There's a Place in Tenterfield.*   *p.156*

20 *Round Three.*   *p.169*

21 *Lemmings and Big Fish.*   *p.179*

Postscript

About the Author

ACKNOWLEDGMENTS

I would like to thank my editor and wife, Anne Lucas; my cover designer and son, Lucas Bradley; and my friend, Martin Brook, without whose eternal optimism and infinite capacity for finding trouble, this journey could never have been the glorious disaster that it was.

Incidentally, for anyone foolish enough to want to recreate our escapade, I have bad news.

It appears that houseboats are no longer available for hire on the Richmond River. All I could find on a quick search of the web was a photo of a half-submerged vessel that had smashed into the marina and sunk.

Martin assures me he was not involved.

CHAPTER ONE
It Wasn't My Fault...

Let me say from the start that it wasn't my fault. I just happened to mention that we'd had some good times on a houseboat on the Myall Lakes. No sane, normal couple, with two kids under the age of three, could possibly take this as an invitation to drive four thousand kilometres to spend a week on a flood-swollen river in a three-tonne steel barge. But then again, I wasn't talking to any sane, normal couple.

I first met Martin and Pammie back in 1981, when Martin was working for the Grundy Organisation as production manager on *Prisoner Cell Block H*. I was the show's original producer but had left the year before, to take up a development contract with Grundy's. It wasn't working out. I'd had an idea for a series about Australian and American diplomats in a fictitious Muslim country, loosely inspired by the Iranian armed takeover of the

Big Fish to Rubber Ducky

American embassy in Tehran in 1979. As it turned out, this proved to be the idea's strength and its weakness. There was early interest from US Cable; in due course, we delivered a script to them. The day after the script arrived, President Carter sent in a Special Forces Operation to rescue the American hostages. It was a spectacular failure, with two marine helicopters crashing in the desert. The result for us was a polite "Love the script but after recent events the American public won't accept any **** series about **** Muslims 'til the **** sea freezes over!" Nearly ten years later we produced the series as *Embassy* for the ABC, but at the time I agreed to return to *Prisoner* for six months, in exchange for being let off the rest of my development contract.

Martin was ideally suited to the role of production manager. Given that the schedule was just about the same week in and week out, the main requirement of his job was to persuade decent, law-abiding citizens that they'd love to let us use their premises as a location; have technicians and actors invade the place from six in the morning until ten at night, doing their best to depict it as a place of depravity and sin, and all for $100 a day.

Martin managed this with a permanently crooked grin

It Wasn't My Fault...

(the legacy of a polio attack as a child) and a look of sweet innocence. He always gave the impression of being totally unworldly and guileless. I can still remember the embarrassment on his face when he and Pammie first told us that although they lived together, they weren't married. They'd said there was something important they needed to tell us and this, apparently, was it.

We were sitting in Pinocchio's restaurant in Toorak at the time. It was the favourite haunt of our then eighteen-month-old son, Lucas, who called the place "Pokey Nose" and insisted on Spaghetti Marinara followed by Pineapple Chunks every time we ate there. At first the owner had objected; lecturing us on what he perceived to be the dangers of such a diet for a toddler. But in the end he gave in and let Lucas have what he wanted, which was what Annie and I always did when it came to food. Annie has this theory that children know what is good for them, and only outside pressures create bad diet. So Lucas was allowed to eat whatever he wanted. The result was that he lived on milk, raw vegetables, fruit, and Spaghetti Marinara until he was four and went to kindergarten, where peer group pressure led him to junk food.

Annie and I didn't know quite how to react to the news. Martin sat there, grinning sheepishly; Pammie, looking expectant. Annie looked at me. I shrugged.
We'd lived together for six years before we got married. And we only got married when we decided to start a family. What did we care if Martin and Pammie didn't want to get married?

"Oh, we want to get married, Bradders" said Martin, seeming upset that I would think otherwise. "The trouble is, I'm already married … to a Parsee."

I wasn't quite sure what a Parsee was. I had a vague memory that they were refugees in India from the Persian Empire. That the men tied pieces of cotton thread around their middle before sitting down to a banquet and only got up when they'd eaten so much that the cotton broke. And that they were all very, very rich.

"They are," Martin agreed. "But I've never seen any of it."

"That's not true," Pammie said. "They were very nice to us."

"You've met them?" I asked Pammie, a bit surprised.

"Yes," said Pammie. "We stayed with them in India on the way back from England."

You can see why I say Martin and Pammie are no sane, normal couple. What sane person would take his girlfriend to visit his current wife's family?

Martin met Pammie for the first time when he visited her orthodontic surgery in London to have his crooked grin straightened out. Apparently it was love at first bite. Martin fell in love as Pammie was forcing a dental plate into his mouth in an attempt not only to re-align his jaw, but his spine as well. Actually, I can understand this. Having an attractive woman astride you, holding an instrument of torture in her hand is a real turn on for a certain type of Englishman, although I'm not sure that Martin went to an English public school. What I don't understand is what Pammie saw as she peered into Martin's mouth that caused her to reciprocate. Mind you, I've never understood why anybody would want to be an orthodontist in the first place, so I guess this will have to remain one of life's little mysteries.

Whatever it was, when Pammie's time in London came to an end and she prepared to return to Melbourne, Martin decided to accompany her. And here's where it gets really strange. Not only did Martin leave his wife in London and accompany his new love to Australia, he decided to drop in on his in-laws on the way. And Pammie went with him. To me this demonstrates a dangerous disregard for personal safety that should have set the alarm bells ringing. The misadventures they had on the way also indicated a decided lack of pre-planning.

On one occasion they stayed in a new hotel in Kashmir that had produced a wonderfully coloured sales brochure but forgotten to finish the building. The walls and the roof were there, but not the plumbing. Arriving hot and sweaty, all Pammie wanted was a bath; all she found was a large tub with two pipes in the wall where the taps should be and sunlight shining through the pipes. Martin was onto the phone immediately.

"Your brochure promises hot and cold running water," he said.

"We have hot and cold running water, Sir," the Concierge assured him. "If you would only be so good as to wait just a few minutes. Everything in the brochure, we have."

Martin and Pammie waited.

Sure enough, a few minutes later, the sound of bare feet came pattering along the balcony. Cold water suddenly gushed through one of the pipes into the bath followed by hot water, gushing through the other pipe; then silence, followed by the sound of running feet again. Martin and Pammie looked out onto the balcony to see a boy disappearing into the distance, carrying two buckets: one for hot, one for cold. Hot and cold running water.

The experience would have caused most sane, normal people to start looking for a hotel that had actually finished being built. Not Martin and Pammie. While Pammie attempted to immerse herself in the two inches of water now in the bath, occasionally hurrying to the far end of the tub to avoid more hot water as it was flung through the pipe, Martin set about seeing what else in the brochure he could find that the hotel could not deliver. He thought he'd found it in the room service menu. Thirty pages long, with full Indian and European cuisine. Having satisfied himself that the hotel kitchen was as incomplete as their bathroom, Martin again phoned the Concierge.

"We'll have Vichyssoise and Duck a l'Orange, followed by Crepe Suzettes. A Bottle of Chateauneuf-du-Pape and a jug of dry martinis on the balcony before dinner," said Martin.

"There will be a thirty minute delay, sir." replied the

Concierge, without hesitation. And the phone went dead.

Dressed in bathrobes, Pammie and Martin went out onto the balcony to see how this particular miracle would be achieved. They were just in time to see the boy with the water buckets climb into an ancient taxi. Only this time he was carrying a number of food pots. The taxi drove off. The martinis arrived. Martin and Pammie settled back on the balcony, sipped the martinis, and waited…. and waited.

It was about midnight when the boy returned with the food pots full and a waiter from a restaurant in the next town. As the boy and the waiter rolled in the trolley and started to lay out a table on the balcony, Martin and Pammie finished their second jug of dry martinis.

"Trouble in the kitchen?" Martin asked.

"The bloody taxi broke down, sir," said the boy.

Martin and Pammie both had diarrhoea the next day, although both insist that it was due to the richness of the French cuisine when they were, by that time, accustomed only to Indian food. Whatever the reason, and despite the fact that the hotel's toilet was on a par with the rest of the plumbing, Martin and Pammie have always agreed that one day they would like to return to that hotel. It is this lemming-like fascination with repeating past mistakes that led me to hesitate when Martin first suggested we should share a houseboat together.

By then it was 1989. For much of the intervening period we'd lost touch because I'd been working in Sydney, but we did return to Melbourne in 1984 so that I could be Best Man at their wedding, a typical Martin and Pammie affair.

First of all, the wedding almost didn't take place because Martin couldn't produce his divorce papers. We persuaded the Vicar (friend of the family) that proof would eventually be forthcoming, so he very kindly decided to ignore the red tape. After the ceremony we moved on to the reception, held in a private home. Martin and Pammie had decided, against all advice, to employ their ancient house cleaner (the cleaner was ancient, not the house) as Drinks Waitress. Clearly nervous at the prospect, the poor woman sought comfort in the bottle; in several bottles actually. As a result, when she carried the champagne out into the reception room for the bridal toast, she bumped into the first of a row of card tables, on which rested one hundred and twenty pieces of bone china; coffee cups, saucers, sugar bowls and cream jugs. I saw her do it. It all happened in slow motion. She stumbled, almost dropped the tray, stuck out a thin arm to balance herself against the table, then staggered on, kicking the table leg as she went. The table leg, which was of the folding variety, buckled inwards; the table started to collapse against the others, setting off a domino effect…

There followed the longest, sustained crash I have ever heard, as each pile of cups, saucers, and bowls slid down the row of tables and shattered on the quarry-tiled floor, The Cleaning Lady/Drinks Waitress stared at the carnage with a confused sense of detachment.

"Do something, Bradders," said Martin.

I put the old lady into a cab, proposed a very rude toast, and announced that coffee would not be served. Nobody seemed to care.

We got together with Martin and Pammie again in 1987 when I returned to Melbourne to run Crawford Productions. Martin, by that time, was producing corporate videos. It was there, on a dark, wet, cold winter's night that we all decided to buy a place in the sun.

Terence Cooper was in town and came to dinner.

Terence had been quite a successful actor. He even played one of the James Bonds in Casino Royale. Later he was voted New Zealand's Best TV Actor.

Despite this, or maybe because of it, he was always extremely belligerent. When he'd phoned to say he was in town for an exhibition of his paintings, it was with some trepidation that we invited him to dinner. We'd always enjoyed his company, and we wanted him to meet Pammie and Martin, but we weren't at all sure how they would get on. Coops had a way of upsetting people at first contact.

To our surprise he was a changed man. The caustic wit was still there. He still drank. But his sarcasm was less vitriolic. Somehow he seemed at peace with the world. He put it down to living in the tropics. He'd bought a place in Cairns in tropical North Queensland; was painting birds and wildlife and making a reasonable living from it. He was content.

In a pleasantly drunken blur, Martin, Pammie, Annie, and I decided that we too, needed a warm, tropical haven in which to live out our days. Of course we weren't so drunk that we'd consider living in Jo Bjelke Peterson's Queensland. Bjelke Petersen had been Premier of

Big Fish to Rubber Ducky

Queensland for twenty years at the time. He was institutionally corrupt and ran what was as close to a police state as could exist in a Western democracy; as proved by the subsequent imprisonment of a significant number of his senior police officers, including the Commissioner. So Queensland was out of the question. Instead, we settled on northern New South Wales and bought a farm in Byron Bay.

When I say farm, it was more of a large, neglected, overgrown, cow paddock at the bottom of a steep-sided valley. We hadn't even settled the title when we received our first fine for noxious weeds from the local council. Thistles grew up to our armpits and the lantana was so rampant that we later discovered a two hundred-metre dry stone wall that nobody even knew was there. We weren't deterred. We'd bought the farm for the future. There was still plenty of time to put it in order. We hired a manager and got him to draw up a plan to turn the paddock into a Macadamia farm. We got a consultant to regenerate the remnant of ancient rainforest also found beneath the lantana. We were all still committed to work in Melbourne but we headed north as often as possible.

The trouble was, the farm had no farmhouse and

finding accommodation in Byron Bay for eight people wasn't easy, especially over the Christmas period. That's when the houseboat idea came up. The Richmond river joins the sea at Ballina, twenty minutes south of the farm. We could live on the houseboat there. Drive up to the farm. I wasn't terribly keen on the idea. Not that I had any premonition of what that houseboat or the Richmond was like. I just didn't fancy the thought of spending a week on a boat with three other adults and four kids. Fortunately, Annie's teenage niece, Rohan, was to be spending Christmas with us. I phoned Martin with the bad news.

"We can't take a houseboat. They're only licensed to sleep eight. There are nine of us."

"No worries," said Martin. "We'll hire two; one for you, one for us. We can have races up the river. Talk to each other on the boat radio. Big Fish to Rubber Ducky. It'll be an adventure."

If only I'd known.

CHAPTER TWO
"Seguimos Adelante" – We continue forward.

Seguimos adelante: it's an expression I've loved since the fourth form of grammar school, when the Latin master suggested that I might like to give up Latin and study Spanish instead. *Seguimos Adelante* was the title of my Spanish text book. I thought it very appropriate. I was going forward…to a new adventure; learning a language spoken in a country I could actually visit, and later did. The Latin master was probably rather more relieved than I was, when I took up his offer. He despaired at having to teach young thugs the intricacies of Latin. So much so that, between lessons, he would hurry back to the common room and sneak a swig of gin to fortify himself. Of course everybody knew about it, but such eccentricity was considered normal for staff at the school. We had a Metalwork teacher who used to fly into fits of anger, pick up red-hot rivets from the forge and hurl them at the

"Seguimos Adelante"

shins of any unfortunate boy who irritated him. The Headmaster regaled bruised or burned boys who complained, with stories of the teacher's war record and the horrific injuries he had sustained in defence of our freedom. He never convinced me. On my last day at school, we dismantled that teacher's motor bike, painted it red, and suspended it from the ceiling of the entrance hall like a giant mobile. We also drove another teacher's car down an embankment, and through the fence onto the tennis courts. Violence begets violence.

Anyway, we set off for Byron Bay or more specifically the Ballina marina on the Richmond river. It was the time of the air pilots' strike, so we had to drive. We travelled in separate cars, and for a very good reason. We'd once travelled all together in a Tarago van, and I made a vow then, never to repeat the experience. Martin and Pammie had chosen that particular moment to potty-train their first-born, young Willie, but he hadn't quite got the knack of it. He did, however, understand the satisfying reaction he would get if he just happened to utter the words:

"I want a wee wee."

"Quick Bradders, pull over, pull over. There's a place."

The Tarago would come to a halt beside some tree in the middle of nowhere. Pammie and Willie would alight and disappear behind the nearest tree. When they re-emerged, Martin would inquire anxiously,

"Did he do it?"

When he did, Martin would congratulate him. When he didn't, which was far more often, Pammie and Will would climb back on the bus and we would drive on… waiting, just waiting, for those inevitable words to be repeated:

"I want a wee wee."

It took us three days to drive from Byron Bay to Sydney, after which we abandoned the Tarago and travelled separately.

This time we decided from the beginning to take four days for the trip, and stop at the Parkes Observatory and the Western Plains Zoo on the way. Annie had suggested this, saying that since we rarely travelled through inland New South Wales, we should see as much as we could along the way. I think she was just trying to slow Martin down. The problem was that Martin had the most highly developed competitive spirit I've ever encountered. He couldn't stand to come second in anything.

"Seguimos Adelante"

Even when we were teaching young Lucas draw poker, Martin would rather cheat than let Luc beat him. And Luc was only six at the time. So it was with driving. We'd set off together but Martin would soon disappear over the horizon. We overcame this by arranging fixed meeting places on the journey. As we reached each stop, Martin would be there, waiting, looking at his watch.

"Where've you been? We've been here for nearly half an hour. We were worried about you."

Of course Martin was now travelling under a handicap: an eleven-month-old baby who had to be fed and changed regularly, and we often drove past their car parked by the side of the road, with Pammie tending to Baby Eddie, Will looking bored, and Martin looking at his watch. Usually, some miles further down the road, Martin's car would again roar past us. Occasionally it wouldn't, and we'd arrive first. Then I'd look at my watch and say,

"Where've you been? We've been here nearly half an hour. We were worried about you."

Martin would have some tale of woe about the delay, inevitably caused by a lack of consideration on the part of the baby who was always losing its bottle or leaving its change bag at the last pit stop, resulting in Martin having to drive back and find it. I thought this was funny but Annie wasn't amused. She knew Martin would try even harder to reach the next meeting place first, and she foresaw the effect it would eventually have on me.

The roads through western New South Wales are pretty good and pretty empty, and although Martin drove quickly, he seemed pretty safe. Of course that was in a car. What neither Annie nor I had anticipated was that Martin's competitive spirit would apply just as much in a three tonne steel houseboat.

So we drove steadily on - 'seguimos adelante' - unaware of what fate had in store for us.

CHAPTER THREE
Is it a House or is it a Boat?

The only person who had given any real thought to the houseboats we were hiring, was our four year-old daughter, Kate. She was having some difficulty coming to grips with the concept of a houseboat.

"Is it a house or is it a boat?" she asked, as we drove along.

"It's a house, but it's on water," Annie explained.

"A house would sink if it was on water," Kate replied,

Annie tried again.

"It's a house, but it's on top of a boat."

"A house'll squash a boat," said Kate.

"It won't," said Annie. "It's a special kind of house, built specially to fit onto a boat."

Kate was unimpressed.

"I want to stay in a hotel," she said.

"No. No. You'll like the houseboat," Annie assured her. "It's just like a hotel."

"Does it have room service?" asked Lucas, whom we'd always taken with us on business trips, so that by the time he was three, he'd been around the world a couple of times and was now considered by his peers to be an expert on room service. Annie told him that of course it didn't have room service, but it did have a T.V.

"A video?" asked Luc.

"No video."

"I want to stay in a hotel, too," announced Luc.

I tried the subtle approach.

"Could you all be quiet? Daddy's trying to concentrate on driving."

Luc looked out of the window.

"Martin's just overtaken us again," he said.

This was the third day of the trip and by now the race with Martin had become a major pre-occupation with Lucas and his older cousin Rohan, who sat on either side of Kate, in the back seat. Every time Martin disappeared over the horizon they'd chant.

"He's getting away, Dad."

"Go faster, Uncle Ian."

I'd bought the brand new Honda Integra a couple of weeks before and I had no intention of racing anybody. Besides, I had Annie sitting beside me, imploring me to let him go and not to encourage the children. For the first two days of the trip I listened to this wise counsel. By the third day, Martin's competitiveness was beginning to get to me.

The first day had been a leisurely drive from Melbourne to Wagga. We'd checked into the motel early and gone swimming in the indoor pool. Despite its location, deep in the basement of the concrete building, the pool wasn't heated, and I had to stand waist deep in freezing water as Kate dove off the side and swam out to me. Have you noticed how small children never seem to feel cold? After half an hour of this I retired to our bedroom, wrapped myself in a blanket and had a stiff scotch. Annie did the same, even though she hadn't put so much as a toe in the water.

The second day was even more relaxed. We stopped at the Observatory in Parkes, and then drove on to the Western Plains Zoo, near Dubbo, where we stayed in a motel with a sensible, sunny, outdoor pool, and a terrific restaurant. By this time I was beginning to feel quite civilised, although Martin was now overtaking us at least five times a day.

The third day was more difficult. It's a little less than two thousand kilometres from Melbourne to Byron. Five hundred kays a day on good country roads is very easy, but at some point we had to cross the Great Dividing Range that separates the entire eastern coast of Australia from the inland. We had decided on two easy stages to Wagga and Dubbo, then crossing the mountains between Glen Innes and Grafton on the third day.

By the time we approached Armidale, Martin had already overtaken me four times. We'd got away from the motel first, but Martin overtook us before we got to breakfast at Coonabarabran. In fact he'd overtaken us twice. The baby must have left its bag at the motel again. He overtook us again before lunch at Tamworth, and again after lunch, as we drove on to Armidale.

"If he has to keep overtaking us, he's not getting there any quicker than we are, is he?" said Annie, but the cries of disappointment from the kids in the back seat as I pulled over to let Martin pass yet again, played on my mind. As we drove into Armidale, a desperate plan was forming. The New England Highway to Glen Innes and

Is it a House or a Boat?

Grafton lay ahead; distance, Glen Innes 97 kilometres, Grafton 258 kilometres. To the right was another road. It didn't have a name. It just said, Grafton 201 kilometres; 57 kilometres less. We'll take that route, I decided. Arrive in Grafton before Martin. Be sitting in the motel pool, sipping champagne, as Martin drives in, hot and dusty. The kids were all for it but Annie was doubtful.

"The road doesn't have a name," she pointed out.

"Look on the map," I said. "Is it sealed road all the way?"

"How can you tell?"

"Is it one thick red line all the way?"

"There's a little bit with two thin red lines," said Annie

"How much?"

"Ten - fifteen kays, maybe." Annie said.

"Well let's take it," I said. "How bad can ten kays of dirt road be?"

At first the road was perfect; long, empty, straight and heading across the central plains. But the names on the map should have sounded a warning: Wollombi Falls, one of Australia's highest waterfalls; Ebor Falls, Upper *and* Lower; and as we crossed the mountain's peak, Clouds Creek. But my real favourite was the descent down the other side, on the dirt road into Nymboida, home of the famous white-water Canoe Slalom Course. At this point the mountainside is almost perpendicular. The road is a series of one hundred and eighty degree turns, as it switchbacks down the mountain. The surface is made up of huge boulders strewn on loose earth. I don't think a grader had been through on the road for years. In fact, I am not sure a grader could have got through. Even the kids were stunned into silence as I gripped the steering wheel, and descended into the gloom. The road was on the eastern side of the mountains and was so steep that in the late afternoon, even at the height of summer, it was shrouded in darkness.

I believe the rainforest beside the road is beautiful. Some of the views are spectacular, they say. I never saw them. All I saw was the dirt track twisting and turning before me. It wasn't a matter of getting to Grafton before Martin now; it was a matter of getting to Grafton alive.

I don't remember breathing between the time we started the descent and the time we reached Nymboida, but I suppose I must have. My eyes stuck out like organ stops. I suddenly felt very tired. We never travelled that road again.

I drove on in shocked silence but kids are amazingly resilient.

"That was *awesome*," said Rohan, to a chorus of agreement from the others in the back.

By the time we'd reached the coastal plain, and were driving alongside Blaxland Creek towards Coutts Crossing and Grafton, they were already doing their calculations. The journey from Armidale to Grafton had taken us a little under three hours, although it seemed longer. The road from Glen Innes to Grafton, which Martin was driving, also had to cross the mountains, on sealed road admittedly, but Martin might not have arrived yet. It was with an air of excitement that we drove into our motel.

We'd never stayed in Grafton before. We've never stayed there since. I am sure there are good motels in Grafton. This wasn't one of them. We'd selected the place from the RACV Accommodation Guide which had given it three stars but it must have been a long time since any RACV inspectors had visited the place to check the rating. The construction was fibro board and in both our room and the kids' room, previous tenants had punched holes in the wall. The décor was reminiscent of the troubles in Ireland: Green table and chairs clashed with vivid Orange bedspreads. The curtains were the same shade of orange. Even worse, they were so narrow that no matter how you arranged them, the remains of the summer sunlight poured in through the gap between the edge of the curtains and the edge of the window. And the curtains themselves were made of a kind of see-through nylon.

The motel's restaurant was closed. After all, as the manager pointed out, it was New Year's Eve. If we wanted to, we could eat at the local pub but we'd have to drive around there to book; the motel rooms didn't have phones. The pool was closed for repair. We stared into the big, dry, cracked hole; the cracks no doubt caused by those same tenants who'd taken it upon themselves to ventilate the rooms. We agreed this was the worst motel we'd ever stayed at. There was but one saving grace. We'd got there before Martin.

Supposedly in compensation for the missing swimming pool, the motel had recently acquired a spa, which stood on a patch of worn grass beside the empty pool. While I walked around to the local pub to book a table for dinner and buy a couple of bottles of cold champagne, the kids got into their swimmers to try out the spa. By the time I returned, the kids were standing around, wet, shaking, and almost hysterical with laughter. In all fairness, the motel manager had said they'd recently acquired the spa. He didn't say they'd merely sat it on the grass, not secured to the ground in any way. The result was that you could sit in the spa. You could fill it with water. But if you actually switched on the jets, the whole thing would suddenly start to shake and shudder, like a very badly loaded washing machine. For young bodies like Luc and Rohan and the even younger Kate (who has always been attracted to the wildest rides at Seaworld or Disneyland) this was all great fun. For tired old television executives like me, it looked very uncomfortable. I declined their entreaties to try it. I'd have a shower in my room instead, thank you. But ...

"Why not offer Martin a relaxing spa when he arrives?"

Martin should have suspected something. As he drove into the motel, everybody was so solicitous. How was the drive? Wasn't the road terrible? How did Willie and the Baby cope? Martin must be exhausted. The motel wasn't up to much but we'd booked dinner at the local pub.

We'd all had a relaxing spa. Why doesn't Martin get into his swimmers; have a nice glass of champagne in the spa?

When the whole family emerged in their swimming cossies, Annie insisted that Martin get into the spa first, and we would only hand Baby Eddie to him when the spa was working, so Eddie wouldn't be frightened by the bubbles. I think Pammie must have realised something was up because she clutched Eddie to her bosom, told Martin to get into the spa and, like Annie, took a step backwards, holding on firmly to Will's chubby little hand. Rohan gave Martin his glass of champagne, and Lucas stood with his finger poised over the power switch. Martin took a sip of the champagne, leaned back with a sigh of pleasure, closed his eyes…and Luc turned on the spa.

Martin's weight actually prevented the side of the spa he was sitting on from leaving the ground. But the other side of the spa leapt fully thirty centimetres into the air and water under pressure shot up through the centre of it raining down on Martin and everybody else standing around. Martin, shaking violently and clutching the side of the spa with one hand and his glass of champagne with the other, yelled:

"Switch it off! Switch it off!"

But everybody, including Pammie, had collapsed with laughter. In fact it was the first time I saw Baby Eddie actually let out a belly laugh.

When Lucas had switched off the power and he and Rohan had helped Martin out of the spa and wrapped him in a towel, Martin, Pammie, Annie, and I sat under the verandah, sipping champagne and watching the kids take it in turns to 'ride the rapids' in the spa. Sadly for them, because the spa rocked so violently each time it was switched on, it gradually dug a hole for itself in the ground on which it sat, so that the rocking grew less and less violent and the kids grew less and less enchanted. What use was a spa that *didn't* rock around violently every time you switched it on? The kids eventually joined us for a cold drink, and everyone agreed that Martin's ride in the spa had been the best. Martin looked at me with his crooked grin.

"You bastard, Bradders," he said.

I looked as innocent as I could.

"What makes you think it was my idea?" I asked.

"I still remember the speech you made at our wedding," Martin replied.

Big Fish to Rubber Ducky

New Years Eve in the Grafton pub was a reasonably enjoyable affair, although the chef was one of those country chefs who thinks making everything as fancy as possible is a sign of sophistication. Personally, I can take my Loin of Lamb without the Apricots, Pine Nuts, and a Dijon Mustard Crust with Parmesan Cheese, but everybody had a good time. I remember we argued late into the night, when Rohan remarked that in ten years time we would be celebrating the new millennium, and I said that it depended on whether the calendar started at nought or one, when Jesus was born. Most people would argue it is the former, in which case the new millennium wouldn't actually start until the year 2001. Alternatively, what if Jesus was born on December the 25th and automatically became one on January 1st, in the same way that all thoroughbred racehorses in the Northern Hemisphere automatically become one on January 1st, even if they were born just a week before?

I can't remember the outcome of that discussion. All I can remember is being woken very early by a blinding orange light. Our bedroom faced east and what dawn sunlight didn't stream straight through the gap between the curtains and the window's edge was filtered, but not stopped, by the orange nylon. Everybody seemed to suffer the same rude awakening, so we decided on an early start.

This time, Annie insisted that I let Martin drive off first. She also insisted that I didn't take any shortcuts. Since the kids slept in the back of the car until we reached Macdonald's in Ballina for breakfast, they didn't care. It was still only ten o'clock when we finished breakfast. Three hours until we could take control of the houseboats or, as it turned out, they could take control of us. We decided to fill in the time by visiting the farm we'd accidentally bought, fifteen months earlier.

CHAPTER FOUR
The Best Laid Plans.

After Terence Cooper had finished his Melbourne exhibition and returned to Cairns with a fat sales cheque, we set about planning the search for our place in the sun; the search which eventually led to the purchase of our farm. By our standards, it was organised with the precision of a military exercise. We had already agreed that we didn't want to live under Bjelke Peterson, so Queensland was out of the question. This left us with northern New South Wales; but where in northern New South Wales?

Pammie, who is one of those irritating women who has a perfect golf swing, teaches skiing and horse riding, and can beat you at every sport you play, insisted that if we were moving north we had to live on the coast, so she could learn to surf.

Annie, who is a great cook and has never played sport in her life, insisted that it had to be somewhere she could buy the herbs, spices and range of vegetables and fruits you find in the produce markets of Melbourne.

Martin, who isn't a great cook, insisted it also have a range of good restaurants.

And I insisted that it had to be within an hour's drive of an airport so that if any business opportunities arose, we could be on a plane, to Sydney or Melbourne or even overseas, within twenty four hours.

Everyone agreed we needed a large block of unspoilt land, far from High Rise Developments or the sort of Suburban Sprawl that engulfs the coast of south-eastern Queensland and the southern capital cities.

All this restricted us to an area from the Queensland border to as far south as Yamba: the Northern Rivers region. By sticking a pin in the map about half way down, we settled on Byron Bay as the base from which we would extend our search, and with this in mind, we set about arranging the trip north.

It was 1988. I was CEO of Crawford Productions and Crawford's was owned by Ariadne. Ariadne also owned the luxury development of Sanctuary Cove on the Gold Coast, although this being just after the stockmarket crash of November '87, they were already trying to sell both enterprises. In the meantime, as an Ariadne employee, I had access to a terrific accommodation deal at the Hyatt in Sanctuary Cove. So we decided to fly to Coolangatta, spend a few days of luxury there, and then drive down the coast into New South Wales.

It was on this trip that we hired the infamous Tarago van, since there were eight of us travelling, including Kate's nanny, Maxie. We had no inkling, of course, that Willie's potty training would become such an important part of the trip. It was also not such a good idea, in retrospect, to spend a few days in the most modern and luxurious hotel in Australia (at the time) before looking for a rustic retreat. Comparisons were bound to make northern New South Wales seem a little basic. Even at Sanctuary Cove we got our first indication that living outside a major city in Australia would have its drawbacks. As I said, the hotel was brand new. Not so new that it hadn't been finished like Martin and Pammie's hotel in India, but the staff were obviously still being trained, and the service didn't quite match up to the surroundings. I'd describe it as friendly and enthusiastic, rather than professional and unobtrusive. They all looked like children and said "Fantastic!" a lot, whenever you spoke to them,

"Faaan-*tas*-tic!"

Not that this bothered us to begin with. We played with the kids on the artificial beach that surrounds the main swimming pool, soaked in the hot spa, which was fed by water bubbling down a series of colonnaded terraces from yet another pool. But it did become a problem on our last night at the hotel. We were joined by Stan Walsh and his family. Stan was working at the nearby Warner Brother studios. His wife, Sherri, and young Stephanie were spending the school holidays with him. Since our two families had virtually grown up together, it was a good opportunity for a reunion. The adults decided to leave the kids with the nanny and a set of videos and pizza from room service, and try out The Grange, the hotel's Premier Restaurant. We asked the staff about the restaurant. They all reckoned it was "Faaan-*tas*-tic!"

With the immaculate timing characteristic of so many of our adventures with Pammie and Martin, this was the very night that a Japanese consortium had arrived to buy the hotel. To meet with the owners of the many villas that surround the Sanctuary Cove Golf Course, they had chosen the Private Dining Room in The Grange, because the meeting was to be followed by a formal dinner.

When we arrived in the restaurant, unaware of all this, it was empty, except for a gaggle of immaculately dressed and nervous young waiters, lined up, waiting for the Main Event. They must have been thankful to have something to do at last because the attention we received was overwhelming. We were ushered to our table. The waiters outnumbered us two to one. While one waiter laid a napkin in each of our laps, another handed each of us a menu and a third waiter took our drink orders. This was perfect, if a bit over the top.

About half an hour after we sat down, a second group arrived to dine. This meant that we now had only one waiter per person instead of two, but we weren't complaining. We all watched, bemused, as our entrée orders arrived, each one carried by our personal waiter, on a silver salver under a silver domed lid. The salvers were placed on the table, the waiters lined up behind each chair and upon a signal from their Captain, simultaneously lifted all the lids to reveal the first course, beautifully presented, and very tasty. We were impressed.

The food was good. The wine was good. The service was maybe still a bit over the top, but very good.

Then the shareholders meeting in the Private Dining Room next door finished, and their dinner began. In an instant, every waiter disappeared. Our main courses didn't arrive. The wine dried up. We had been deserted.

The staff had clearly been taught that all meals must be brought to the table simultaneously, not plate by plate. All diners must *simultaneously* savour the moment the silver lids are removed, and the chef's creations revealed, to gasps of delight. This meant that they needed at least one waiter for each two diners (they later revealed their great dexterity by removing two silver domes each, one on either side) and all the waiters were busy showing off their expertise in the Private Dining Room next door.

After about an hour, a window of opportunity opened. When the hordes next door had been served their entrees, fussed and fawned over, and were tucking into whatever it was they had ordered, the army of waiters reappeared carrying the silver salvers. Once again, they performed their simultaneous removal trick. This time we stared down at the dried, blackened remains of what had once been our main courses. I don't think anyone had told the chef there'd be a traffic jam. I assume he had prepared the meals when ordered, as usual, and they had sat broiling under some sort of warming device until the waiters had time to serve them up.

"This is burnt!" I barked.

The waiters, who were already beating a hasty retreat to the kitchen with the silver domes in hand stopped, and stared at each other in confusion. Could they pretend they hadn't heard me and scurry out? Eventually, the most senior of the waiters returned to the table, while the others made good their escape.

I told the waiter I wanted my meal replaced. I also wanted the red wine we had ordered over an hour ago. I asked the rest of the people at the table if they'd like their meals replaced, but they looked at the dried mess in front of them, considered their hunger, silently calculated how long it would take for the new meals to arrive, if ever, and declined my offer. They were right. When my main course re-appeared 45 minutes later it was still dried up and overcooked.

By this time the staff had given up any pretence. We didn't see them for another hour. When the desserts arrived, some time after eleven o'clock, they appeared one by one, and looked suspiciously like the desserts that were available in the cafeteria in the hotel foyer.

I asked for the bill. When it arrived it was for literally hundreds of dollars. Not only had they charged us for the wine we'd ordered and never received, but they'd also managed to include the wine bill from the only other occupied table in the main restaurant.

I stared at the waiter, hovering, waiting for my credit card to appear.

"Do you have a Maitre'd?" I asked politely.

"I'm not sure, sir," he said. "I could ask?"

"Please," I said.

"It'll probably be a long wait," said Martin. "Do you reckon I could have some Earl Grey tea while we're waiting?"

We sat and waited for the appearance of the Maitre'd, and the Earl Grey tea. Eventually a mannequin appeared in a dinner suit, looking like an extra from *The Young and The Restless*.

"Can I help you, sir?" he asked, managing to avoid looking at my face as he spoke. I told him,

"This is the worst restaurant I have ever been to in my life, I said. "This is the worst food, the worst service..

I can't tell you whether it's the worst wine, because our bloody order still hasn't turned up even though you've charged us for it. There are only two tables in the restaurant yet you've managed to confuse the bills, and charged us for wine ordered by the other table as well. If you can't run a restaurant better than this, you should close the bloody place down. And if you think I'm paying for this rubbish, you're out of your mind!"

Actually I ranted on a lot worse than this, but you get the idea.

The Maitre'd waited to make sure I'd finished. He looked directly at me for the first time, and smiled.

"Thank you for sharing your thoughts with us, sir," he said…and turned, and walked away, leaving the bill on the table.

We all sat there, speechless. By this time a younger waiter, who looked like he came out of *Neighbours* had arrived with Martin's Earl Grey tea in a silver teapot, with a silver milk jug and sugar bowl, a single fine bone china cup and saucer, a silver spoon and a silver tea-strainer; all immaculately presented on a silver tray.

As we watched, mesmerised, he carefully placed the cup and saucer in front of Martin, placed the tea strainer onto the cup, and poured the tea from the pot. Instead of the tea going through the strainer, it welled up and flowed over the sides of the cup, over the saucer, and onto the white linen tablecloth, forming a large brown stain. The waiter picked up the tea strainer, put it up to the light, and stared at it in disgust.

"Faaan-*tas*-tic!" he said. "They've forgotten to punch the bloody holes in the tea strainer. Wouldn't it cap off a perfect night?"

We returned to the rooms, where unfortunately the kids had polished off all the pizza and everyone felt too tired and weak to order room service. The following morning, I received a call from the hotel manager, apologising for the meal, agreeing that we shouldn't pay for it, and offering us a free meal in the restaurant as compensation. I declined the offer. I didn't share Martin's lemming-like fascination for revisiting past disasters. Besides, we were going to find our place in the sun.

CHAPTER FIVE
A Place with a View.

The main problem with eight-seater people movers like Taragos, is that they carry eight people. On a hot day the air-conditioning just isn't up to it, and the two-litre engine really strains to get up the hills. The main advantage is that you ride very high. Peering over the roofs of passing cars, you can see for miles without having to stop and get out. From this vantage point we drove over the New South Wales border, turned left at Kingscliff, and headed down the coast road in search of Valhalla. For miles we followed the coastline, covered in sand dunes, untidy scrub, and tidy suburban houses. This wasn't for us.

The road turned inland and we didn't see the coast again until Byron Bay. As soon as we got there we knew we had found The Place. Lush rolling hills overlooked the town and the famous Cape Byron lighthouse; superb surfing beaches for Pammie; greengrocers, delicatessens and markets for Annie; thirty restaurants, one for every one hundred people then living in the town, for Martin; and Ballina airport just twenty minutes away for me. We made a desultory attempt later to drive down the coast as far as Yamba, but our hearts weren't in it. We'd already decided Byron was the place.

The problem was finding a suitable property. The developers had taken over the coastal strip around Byron and prices even back then were terrifying. To the north and south, national parks prevented further sprawl, and inland development had been halted by the wetlands which separate the coast from the escarpment. Our attention was drawn to the top of the escarpment where the St Helena ridge rises above the town, commanding a view for miles up and down the coast; north-west to Mount Warning in the Nightcap Range and south-east to the lighthouse. We agreed this was the place to buy. Unfortunately, we weren't the first to come to that conclusion.

"Properties rarely become available on The Ridge," the Real Estate Agents told us, and tried to sell us charming rural retreats like the one on Cemetery Road, complete with its own Birthing Hut, built without planning permission by the hippies who had just vacated the place leaving behind a pile of rubbish and the smell of incense. Martin has a morbid fear of death and wasn't going to live anywhere called Cemetery Road, and Pammie, then already five month's pregnant with Baby Eddie, certainly wasn't going to give birth in a mud-floored, bark hut. We left our phone number with all the local agents, told them to call if ever a property became available on the ridge, and headed south to Sydney in the Tarago. Having already read a bit about that particular trip you will understand why, by the time we got there and caught the plane back to Melbourne, the idea of buying a place together had lost much of its charm for me.

To be honest I'd forgotten all about it and was attending yet another television market in Cannes, when I received a fax from Annie announcing the sale of a hundred-acre property, by auction, on the ridge. The auction was due to take place before I got back from overseas. I called Annie and told her to contact Stan Walsh, who was still working at Warner Bros., on the Gold Coast, just an hour or so from Byron Bay.

Could he drive down and look at the place? He did and the news came back.

"Stan says to buy. But we've got a problem. The agent says somebody has already offered twenty-one hundred dollars an acre. Martin thinks we should offer twenty-two".

The Cannes markets (MIPCOM, MIPTV) are held twice a year in the northern spring and autumn. They are much like the better known Cannes Film Festival really, except it's colder and the women wear more clothes. They are designed to allow all the North European television executives to get a bit of sunshine before and after the northern winter, when the days are so short that everybody travels to and from work in the dark; and to allow all the French hotel and bar owners to double their prices, so they can make enough money to close up shop for the winter and head for Tahiti. During the markets, even in the 80s, a single room cost thirteen hundred francs a night. A large scotch on La Croissette could set you back nearly ninety francs. Money ceases to have any real value.

"Why offer just twenty-two hundred dollars an acre?" I asked Annie from my very expensive Cannes' hotel room, speaking on my even more expensive hotel telephone. "We'll probably just get ourselves into a bidding war. Offer twenty-four hundred an acre; a pre-emptive bid".

The sellers accepted the offer immediately. But it wasn't until closer to Christmas that we came to understand why. We only had a spare weekend, so just the four adults and Lucas flew up to Byron Bay to view our property for the first time. We'd only ever seen Byron on clear winter days. In summer, the area is subject to quite violent electrical storms. We arrived as one of these storms was gathering. Even at midday the place was in semi-darkness. The cloud was so low that as we got out of the hire car on the St Helena ridge we were surrounded by a thick fog, and condensation formed on our breath. If there was a view, we couldn't see it. On both sides of the road, the land disappeared into the gloom. Annie and I were all for heading to the motel, having a drink and a good meal, and hoping the sun would be shining the following day. Pammie was made of sterner stuff.

I remember her telling me once that her father, who was about five foot high, was one of the pioneers who opened up the Victorian Snowfields before the war.

When she was a child, the family trekked into Mount Hotham each year, before there was even a road there, carrying all their supplies on their backs. Wading through snow up to their armpits, spending their winters in a hut without electricity or running water. This was the spirit which led her over the barbed wire fence and onto the farm.

"Come on Bradders, we've come all this way, we might as well see the place."

I might still have resisted, but Pammie was by now a full eight months pregnant. I was led on, not by any false sense of chivalry but by the certain knowledge that she would never let me forget it, if she trekked the farm while I waited in the car.

Gingerly, Martin, Annie, Lucas, and I followed Pam, as the land fell away rapidly before us. We'd hardly gone ten yards before Martin was already wondering aloud how Pammie would get back up the hill "in her condition". Pammie was in the middle of admonishing him when she let out a shriek. Some unknown creature had lumbered past her in the gloom, so close that she could feel the heat of its breath on her face.

"It was a cow," said Annie.

"How do you know?"

"Because I just stood in some cow shit."

As we descended into the valley below the clouds, we could see that Annie was right. A herd of cows was grazing on the land, picking their way through the tall thistles, lantana and camphor laurel trees that seemed to be everywhere. Camphor laurels are considered to be noxious weeds in the Northern Rivers. Suddenly, Pammie stopped and said we shouldn't go any further.

"Why not?" I asked. "We might as well see all of it, now."

"Because I'm stuck in a bog," she said.

Martin and I pulled Pammie free with some effort, then Martin kindly let me retrieve one of Pammie's boots which had stayed stuck in the bog. He also let me push Pammie back up the hill towards the road. Even then I am not sure how she managed it. I thought for a while she was going to have the baby there and then. Later we named that hill Heartbreak Hill. At the time we were all too out of breath to speak, which was probably just as well. I didn't want anybody reminding me that I was the one who'd suggested offering twenty four hundred dollars an acre.

We drove down to Byron township in silence and blinding rain. Pammie and Annie commandeered the showers in our respective motel rooms. Martin and I had a scotch and I phoned Stan Walsh at the studios in Queensland.

"How's the farm, mate?" he asked cheerfully.

"A bit of a surprise," I said. "When you phoned Annie, why didn't you mention the bog?"

"What bog?"

"The bog in the middle of the farm. And while you were at it, why didn't you mention the camphor laurels and the lantana? And the thistles and the cow shit?"

"I didn't see any cow shit."

"Mate, you couldn't have stepped onto the property without seeing the cow shit. You couldn't have stepped onto the property without stepping *in* the cow shit."

"Oh, I didn't step onto the property," said Stan. "I thought you wanted a place with a view, so I just drove up the road and looked over the escarpment. You've got a terrific view of the lighthouse, mate."

At the time I could have happily throttled Stanley. Fortunately he was nearly a hundred miles away.

Instead, we had a great meal at the old Figtree restaurant, while outside the midsummer thunderstorm ripped open the sky with great shards of forked lightening.

We all slept very soundly that night, as the rain drummed down, and when we woke up, the sun was shining. We drove back up to the farm. Stan was right. There was a fantastic view from the road. In the sunshine the thistles didn't seem so high. Heartbreak Hill didn't look so steep. Instead of threatening, misshapen monsters, the cows just looked like…cows. The only nasty surprise was a letter in the box at the gate, from the local council: a fine for having noxious weeds on the place.

And I'd always thought country people were a bit slow.

CHAPTER SIX
Something for Posterity.

The farm we saw when we drove up after breakfast in Ballina was almost unrecognizable. A road now ran down one side of Heartbreak Hill to a manmade level area, on which stood the new, steel-bonded shed that housed our two tractors. The lantana and the smaller camphor laurel trees had been bulldozed away. The large red scars in the side of the hill where the land had subsided, had been graded into smooth, even contours, and up and down the slopes were thousands of small macadamia plantings.

Macadamia trees are grafted onto rootstock like the vines in vineyards: a good nut-producing variety of macadamia, grafted onto a disease-resistant stock. In the late eighties, the Macadamia industry went through a bit of a decline, so it was easy to buy eighteen-month-old graftings, and plant them on the property. Well, it wasn't actually that easy to plant them. Much of our land was too steep to harvest, so on the steep bits we'd planted about ten thousand hardwoods, close together. These would eventually form a canopy over the non-arable land, cutting out the sunlight, and preventing the proliferation of noxious weeds... and noxious fines from the council. What land was level enough to plant macadamias was strewn with heavy boulders, and we planned to use these boulders to build a dam across the bog. In the end we had enough to build three dams, so the bottom of the valley became a series of ponds that were already attracting the local bird life.

It was on clearing the land at the head of the valley that we had made the most exciting discovery. Hidden under the lantana was not only a dry stone wall, but also the remnants of an ancient rainforest. When the Europeans first discovered the area around Byron Bay they called it The Big Scrub, because it was covered in rainforest. It didn't take long for the timber cutters to move in and fell the giant Red and White Cedars, clearing the smaller scrub to get at the trees they were after. The escarpments south of Byron, known as Cooper's Shoot, and Skinner's Shoot are literally the places where felled trees would shoot down the escarpment, to be loaded onto waiting barges in the bay. Being in an inaccessible valley, we had one of the few remaining patches of rainforest near the coast, and we decided not only to keep it, but to regenerate it by planting the fast growing rainforest trees known as pioneer species. These would form a dark canopy, denying sunlight to the weeds and allowing the three hundred-odd species of rainforest plants, which lay dormant under the weeds, to take hold and grow. By the time these seedlings were strong enough and ready for their share of open sky and sunlight, the pioneer species would be ready to die off.

At the time, our Farm Manager referred to this as a "Rich Man's Folly" when he thought we were out of earshot. He was wrong on two counts. We weren't rich, and nowadays it is accepted that macadamias, being rainforest trees originally, grow better when there is rainforest nearby. We didn't know this at the time of course; our interests were purely aesthetic. Although, after just a year, it had to be said that our rainforest, with its straggly pioneer species surrounded by a mulch of rotting newspaper, looked even worse than when we'd first discovered it. The rest of the farm however, was really beginning to blossom. Each time we visited we took photos from the same vantage points so that, over the years, we built a record of the farm's development. On this occasion, Martin had decided to go one better.

He'd decided to record not only the farm but the entire trip on video. To help him, I stood on the site beside the road where we intended to build a house, lifted him up on my shoulders and slowly turned in a three hundred and sixty-degree circle so that he could take a full panorama of the view.

Have you noticed how even the most spectacular view can look flat and uninteresting on video? To the naked eye, or rather the two naked eyes that give a sense of distance, depth and perspective, the view was and still is, magnificent. Looking at the video afterwards, it was nothing. Martin was disappointed too, and abandoned his plan to record our trip for posterity. However, I think that decision might have had more to do with the footage he shot a little later that day, on his houseboat.

We had eventually reached the marina, and while the staff were explaining the handling of our houseboat to us, the Brookies had gone off to explore their own houseboat, and record the whole adventure. Baby Eddie wasn't walking yet but could crawl at an incredible speed.

Big brother Willie, as three-year-old big brothers are wont to do, thought the best way to stop Eddie scurrying off was to grab hold of one ankle. This had the desired effect but occasionally, if Eddie's ankle was grabbed in full flight, his momentum would continue to carry him forward until his head and body could go no further. Then Eddie would pitch forward, fall flat on his face and let out a scream; more of frustration than pain, but none the less piercing for that.

It was during Pammie's first conducted tour of the houseboat, all lovingly taped by Martin, that in order to demonstrate the wardrobes and the view from the porthole, Pammie was required to temporarily put Eddie down on the bunk. Eddie immediately took off, and it was only Will's swiftness of hand that prevented the baby from launching himself off the bunk. Unappreciative of his brother's concern for his safety, Eddie let out a scream of protest. In the confines of the cabin this sounded even more piercing than usual. Pammie immediately swept the baby up in her arms, and tried vainly to comfort him. As Martin continued to record the episode, Pam admonished Will with the most dire punishment she could think of:

"No more Strepsils for you, young man!"

Will was going through an addiction to Strepsils. He'd first gotten the taste when Martin gave him a Strepsil for a mild sore throat. After a few weeks he'd become an addict, constantly complaining of a sore throat in order to get more Strepsils. Pammie is an orthodontist. She could find no trace of infection. Clearly he ate Strepsils for pleasure, hence the punishment was a very real one to Will. He howled his protest. It wasn't his fault! Pammie, while shushing Eddie, who was still howling, told Willie she'd warned him before about grabbing Eddie's ankle. Martin's plaintive voice could be heard off camera,

"All right, all right, Pammie. This is supposed to be a happy family video."

Pammie glared into the camera and snapped,

"Well, get yourself another family, then!"

After that I don't think the video camera came out of its case again for the whole trip.

CHAPTER SEVEN
This is Our House!

Not that we didn't have our own problems getting onto the houseboat. As we approached the marina, Kate's misgivings about a house sitting on top of a boat returned. We unloaded on the quayside, Annie and Pam drove off to buy provisions for the trip, and I walked across to where the two houseboats were tied up at the marina to show Kate that it was all quite safe. I am not sure who was more suspicious of what we saw. I had expected a little timber houseboat like the ones on Myall Lakes. Light, easy to manoeuvre; basically a caravan on a wooden pontoon, with rubber tyres on the side to stop you bumping into things. Instead, these houseboats were constructed on massive, steel-sided barges. They looked more like pocket battle ships than houseboats.

Luc and Rohan were very impressed. They ran on board one of the houseboats. Jumped up and down on the steel deck, to demonstrate to Kate how safe it was. Kate and I stared at them incredulously; Kate wondering why these steel monsters didn't sink; me wondering how I was going to handle such an unwieldy craft on such a relatively small river.

Gingerly, I picked Kate up in my arms, and with her clinging around my neck so tightly I could hardly breathe, I crossed the gangplank and walked onto the houseboat. Lucas and Rohan ran about, yelling at each new discovery. The two bedrooms; one with bunks, the other so small that one double bed practically filled the room. The bathroom. The shower. A main area, which contained the kitchen, dining room, and wheel house. A divan alongside the dining table, which folded out into another, larger bed. A big cold storage box on the roof apparently doubled as a life raft.

"Why does it need a life raft, if it won't sink?" asked Kate.

"Just regulations." I replied, hoping she wouldn't ask me what regulations were.

Kate was still clinging to me when Annie and Pam returned. Having actually got her onto one of the boats, we decided this one would have to be ours, and I had to let Annie and the other kids carry our bags and supplies on board while I watched, still holding Kate.

When a Deckhand came aboard to give me a quick course on how everything worked, I carried Kate around with me. She just wouldn't let go. Together we listened carefully as the Deckhand explained…. The engine was mounted in a boxed enclosure on the back of the boat. Diesel. Very reliable. Filled with fuel. All I really needed to know was how to switch the fuel line off and on. Anything more complicated, and he advised that I should radio back to base for help.

In the wheelhouse, the engine had a start button. Turn on the key. Press the button. What could be simpler?

The anchor, which was a serious chunk of metal, was operated by an electric winch. I was feeling about as ready as I would ever be to take command, even with Kate still clinging around my neck, when Annie called from the kitchen. The fridge door wouldn't open. The Deckhand walked into the kitchen followed by me, with Kate in my arms. Kate was particularly fascinated by the problem with the fridge. She leaned out, still holding onto my neck, to get a better look at what was going on.

I moved to one side so that the Deckhand wasn't blocking our view, and we could both watch proceedings without Kate throttling me. Even from across the room it was obvious what the problem was. The alcove in which the fridge sat was such a narrow fit that although the fridge stood there looking alright when it was shut, when you tried to open it, the thickness of the door forced it against the side of the alcove, preventing it from opening. The Deckhand couldn't have been more than about eighteen, but he was huge. He grabbed the fridge door and yanked it so hard that the fridge, the alcove, and the whole houseboat seemed to shake. Kate looked at me with a frown on her face. Obviously she didn't approve of this at all.

Annie was explaining that the door was getting jammed up against the wall, and brute force was not going to change that. The Deckhand was undeterred.

"It's just sticking a bit," he said.

He yanked even harder, and this time the door did open. In fact it came away in his hand. He stood there, holding the fridge door by its handle and looking rather bemused. Without a word, Kate released her death grip from around my neck, wriggled free of my grasp, jumped to the floor, and strode across to the Deckhand as he struggled to fit the door back onto the fridge. She came up to just past his knees but this didn't seem to bother her. She shoved him violently in the back.

"This is our house!" she yelled. "Get off!"

And she pushed him again, causing him to stumble backwards and let go of the fridge door. I was too stunned to react. It was Annie who stopped the fridge door from falling onto the floor. Meanwhile Kate continued to shove the Deckhand, forcing him back to the doorway.

"Get off! Get off!" she kept yelling, and he had little option but to obey.

As he reached the doorway, I suggested that the problem was that the fridge was too close to the wall on either side. If it were moved forward an inch or so, the front would be outside the alcove, and there would be nothing to stop the door from opening.

"Right," said the deckhand, and moved forward to shift the fridge.

Kate barred his way, shoved at his legs, and roared:

"This is our house! Get off!"

Annie told Kate not to be rude, but she refused to budge. Blocking the Deckhand's passage to the fridge, shoving at his legs, which must have seemed like tree trunks to her, she was fearless in defence of her home.

I told the Deckhand I thought I could handle the fridge. Relieved, he started to back off the boat with Kate still pushing at him, and worrying him like a miniature cattle dog with a giant Hereford bull. As he stepped off the boat, Kate stood at the head of the gangplank, clenched fists on hips, glaring at him, defying him to step back on board. I manhandled the fridge forward and rehung the door on its hinges. The door rattled a bit but Annie secured the lock with a rubber scrunchy, which Rohan wore in her hair. I went out on deck, where Kate was still glaring at the Deckhand on shore. It wasn't until I had pulled the gangplank on board and fastened the safety rail across that she could be persuaded to leave her post.

Back inside the cabin, Kate looked at the fridge door, satisfied herself that it was fixed, then reverted from being a pit bull terrier to being a little girl again. She threw her arms around her mother's neck, and hugged her.

"You were very fierce," said Annie.

"This is *our* house," said Kate.

Just then the ship's radio crackled into life.

It was Martin.

"Rubber Ducky to Big Fish. Over."

If he'd leant out of his cabin window he could practically have touched our houseboat, but he was getting into the spirit of the adventure. I picked up the microphone.

"Big Fish to Rubber Ducky. We're just about ready to leave. How about you? Over."

"We can't, mate. Our fridge won't work."

Lucas suggested we should send Kate over to sort them out, but this time the problem wasn't so easily fixed. The Manager of the marina had already left for Ballina to get the spare part for the fridge. They had to wait for his return.

Loading up, buying provisions, and persuading Kate to come aboard the houseboat had taken longer than we'd planned and it was now mid afternoon. We had promised the kids we'd moor off an island in the middle of the river for the first night. The map indicated that it was about three hours cruising-time away. We decided to set off ahead of Martin and Pammie, and find a mooring spot.

We'd keep in touch by radio. I turned on the fuel line, turned the key, and pressed the button. The engine roared into life. Rohan and Lucas cast off the mooring ropes. I put the engine into slow reverse, and we backed out onto the river.

Fortunately, there were no boats about and I had plenty of room to manoeuvre, because when I put the engine into slow forward the houseboat, because of its weight, continued to move backwards for about twenty yards before it ran out of momentum and changed direction. But at last we were on our way, moving slowly forward, the engine sounding smooth and low. I lifted Katie up onto the control panel where she sat watching the shore go by, looking at peace with the world.

"This is our house, eh Katie?" I said.

CHAPTER EIGHT
Walking on Water.

Like a lot of rivers in northern Australia, the most interesting thing about the Richmond is the way it changes character. In times of flood, it bursts its banks and inundates large towns like Lismore. At other times, it's a sedate stream, gently running over mud flats and around dangerous rocky outcrops.

If these changes occurred once or twice a year, it wouldn't be too bad. On the Richmond, it happens four times a day. Inland from its mouth at Ballina, the river runs through a flat low-lying plain with virtually no gradient at all, so that the tidal effect extends for miles upstream. On the turn of high tide, when the outgoing tide combines with the normal flow of the river, it is a torrent, running at about fifteen knots. Six hours later, when the incoming tide is stronger than the current, the river actually flows upstream at a more sedate four knots.

Big Fish to Rubber Ducky

In between is a moment when the strength of the incoming tide, and the strength of the river current match exactly, and the river stops. Its surface becomes as smooth as glass. It is silent. It is peaceful. It is beautiful. We started our journey upstream at just that moment.

The hand-drawn river chart supplied by the marina was crude, to say the least. It had no scale whatsoever. The river appeared to be as wide as it was long in places. Horseshoe bends were reduced to gently curves, and navigation buoys, spaced miles apart on the river, appeared to form a constant, straight line on the charts. Not that I was concerned. After all, how can you get lost on a river? You sail upstream. Then you sail downstream. Of course, this does assume that the river always runs in the same direction.

The charts said you kept the navigation buoys on your starboard going upstream, so I set the houseboat on a course aiming a little to the left of the only buoy I could see, and relaxed. Lucas was anxious to take the wheel, and I couldn't see any reason why not. I told him to just hold a steady course to the left of the buoy, and took Kate up onto the roof with Annie.

It was idyllic. The silence was broken only by the

gentle chug of the engine and the 'plop' of fish as they leapt out of the water and fell back again. Cormorants were fishing across the river. Alongside us, pelicans flew in to settle on the water, where they bobbed on the wake made by the houseboat.

I have always been fascinated by pelicans. It seems to me that God ran out of material when he was making them; a bit like hyenas or African hunting dogs. God obviously started at the beak or the jaws, as the case may be, added a head and neck to match, and then suddenly realising he'd overdone it somewhat, stuck the lot onto a ridiculously small body.

In flight, pelicans look regal; when they land, they look like circus clowns. Because of my particular fascination, I was focused on the pelicans; especially one, which sat motionless on the water, near the boat. I marvelled at how it could remain so still. It was as if it was standing there. Then it dawned on me. It *was* standing there. The pelican was standing in about six inches of water, and so were we.

I ran to the back of the houseboat. The propeller was churning up a long wake of mud behind us. I yelled down to Lucas to stop the engine.

The engine stopped. The houseboat stopped. I waited for the current to carry us off the mudflats. There was no current.

We didn't move an inch.

I scrambled down to the wheelhouse where Lucas was telling his cousin it wasn't his fault. I agreed. It was the chart's fault. What else could I say? Nine-year-old boys idolise their fathers; I could hardly admit it was *my* fault. Anyway, what did it matter who was to blame? The problem now was getting off the mud. It was then that I noticed a terrible flaw in the construction of the houseboat.

Running back from the wheelhouse, past the kitchen and dining area, was a passageway leading to the rear of the houseboat. On one side of the passageway was a bedroom, and on the other, the bathroom. This blocked any view out of the boat on either side. At the end of the passageway was another bedroom, running across the width of the houseboat, blocking any view out the back. Standing in the wheelhouse, you could only see forward.

Watching the pelicans walking on water just ahead of the houseboat, I was pretty sure we didn't want to go that way; but if I reversed, would I be heading into even shallower water? Into the bank? Into Martin's houseboat? I had no idea.

I solved the problem by climbing back onto the roof with Rohan, and searching out the nearest bit of blue water. By this time I'd worked out that blue water was deep, and brown water was mud. I went below again. Rohan stayed on the roof of the boat, pointing in the direction of the blue water. Lucas stood on deck outside the wheelhouse, looking up at Rohan, and pointing in the same direction. I put the engine into slow reverse, and attempted to steer the houseboat in the general direction in which both Lucas and Rohan were pointing.

All this time, Annie helpfully stood at the back of the houseboat yelling that the propeller was still churning up mud. I politely explained to Annie that we had two choices. The propeller could churn up mud or we could spend our entire bloody holiday stuck on the mudflats. Had we waited an hour, the incoming tide would have lifted us gently off the mud and floated us upstream, but I didn't know that at the time.

After about fifteen minutes, and dripping with sweat, I managed to manoeuvre the houseboat into blue water again and put the engine into slow ahead.

The houseboat continued to reverse for a while, shuddered, then started moving forward. Giving the marker buoy a wide berth on our right, we headed uneventfully on to the island where we planned to moor for the night.

Annie has a theory about men and boats. She thinks you can put the most reasonable, intelligent man in charge of a boat, and he will immediately turn into a tyrant. She thinks that Captain Bligh and Captain Queeg were probably perfect fathers and husbands when they were at home. But once aboard ship, they became demented. She first formed this theory as I tried to manoeuvre the houseboat off the mudflats. She had it confirmed when we tried to moor for the night.

Having moored houseboats before, I knew the rules. You face the boat up into the current, drop anchor, and let the boat drift back until the anchor takes hold on the bottom of the river, and you can switch off the engine. That's what's supposed to happen. In practice, it is rather more difficult, and it certainly was in this case. For a start, the design of the houseboat again caused problems. The wheelhouse was at the front of the boat, where it should be. The anchor was right in front of the wheelhouse, where it should be. But the only door leading from the wheelhouse to the anchor was half way back down the houseboat, near the dining area. Unless you were Usain Bolt, it was impossible to handle the wheel, and lower the anchor at the same time.

This was definitely a two-person job.

At first we tried it with me at the wheel, and Annie handling the winch on the anchor. I aligned the houseboat parallel with the shore beautifully, and yelled to Annie to lower the anchor. Then yelled to Annie to stop the winch. We had let out enough anchor chain and the houseboat, in theory, would soon come to rest. It didn't. When I'd faced the houseboat upstream, I'd forgotten that the tide was now coming in. The current was running upstream, so instead of the houseboat pulling back from the anchor, the tide carried us forward, and we just ran over it, dragging it along the riverbed behind us. I told Annie to pull in the anchor, and we tried again; this time facing downstream, and into the incoming tide. This time, I gave Annie the wheel and I took the anchor winch. It didn't work.

I cannot understand why, when I indicated to Annie that she should turn the wheel a little left, she thought I meant her left, not my left, which was obviously quite different because I was standing in front of the wheelhouse, looking back at her.

I cannot understand why, when I shouted, "That's enough throttle," Annie took it to mean she should cut the throttle completely. It seems perfectly clear to me that it meant she should have held the throttle exactly where it was.

In the end, I had no alternative but to find the key to the lock on the wheelhouse windows, open the windows, and lean through from the front of the boat, and adjust every steering mistake Annie made as we manoeuvred into position. Rather than being thankful for my help, Annie seemed to resent this. If I could do it so much better, she told me, I might as well just do it in the first place. With this, she ushered the kids up onto the roof where they waited, giggling at the cursing and swearing coming from below as I eventually moored the boat, single-handed.

From then on, and for the entire trip, every time I mentioned that it was time to "up anchor" or "drop anchor" everybody would disappear up onto the roof and hide. I thought it was pretty unreasonable really.

CHAPTER NINE
Scotch and Water Don't Mix.

By the time I'd safely moored the houseboat, the sun was already dipping behind the mountains north-west of the river and there was still no sign of the Brookies. We tried calling on the ship's radio but all we got was static. We tried calling the marina with the same result. Eventually, when Annie was preparing dinner, and I was considering whether to take the outboard and dinghy and run downriver to find Martin, their houseboat came into view, moving slowly through the dusk. I got onto the radio.

"Big Fish to Rubber Ducky. We're moored in the lee of the island. Can you see us? Over."

"Where have you been? We've been trying to call you for hours," came the reply.

Martin was so upset; he even forgot to say "Over."

This is when we discovered the third design fault on the houseboats. Radio waves travel in straight lines and there were no relay towers anywhere on the river. Any hill or other obstacle immediately cut off radio contact.

So if you could see the other boat, you could speak to them; but if you were lost, you couldn't. The radio was about as useful as two tin cans on a very long piece of string, and that wasn't the only reason for Martin's bad temper. Apparently their fridge still hadn't been fixed. Being the New Year holiday, all the electrical stores were closed. Pammie was forced to pack all their perishables, including the baby's milk, into the icebox on the roof of the boat where they were kept cool by several large blocks of ice. The marina Manager had assured Martin that the ice would last the four days until our return to the marina, to meet with our manager on the farm, at which time he would have a fridge for them. Martin wasn't impressed.

"Why do these things always happen to me, Bradders?" he said.

We've often wondered the same thing ourselves.

I won't go into the detail of Martin's first effort to moor their houseboat, other than to say that thankfully, it was already dark, so Martin couldn't have seen Luc and Rohan rolling around in hysterics as they listened to the swearing and cursing that came floating across the water. I'd told Martin to turn the boat downstream so that he avoided the mistake I made of trying to anchor with the current. I also told him to take his houseboat past us before anchoring, so that if the anchor didn't hold, the tide would carry him away from us, rather than crashing into us. I even explained the difficulties of trying to handle the wheel and the anchor at the same time. All this good advice obviously didn't help because it was only on the third attempt, and after the houseboat had twice crashed into trees overhanging the bank, that it eventually came to rest and silence fell over the river.

Ignoring the modern convenience of the ship's radio, Annie yelled across the water.

"I've got a curry on the stove and lasagne in the oven for the kids, Pammie. Are you coming over to eat with us?"

"Can I leave Martin behind?" she replied, but I think Pammie was joking because the lights went on in their houseboat and we could see Pammie putting life jackets onto Willie and Baby Eddie, and Martin bringing the dinghy around to the side of the houseboat so they could all get on board. Pammie handed Eddie and Will down to

Martin, climbed down herself and sat in the bow of the boat, clutching Eddie, while Martin started the outboard. Martin stood in the boat, yanked on the starter rope, almost toppled over and steadied himself as the engine coughed twice, and stopped. Martin yanked again. This time the engine didn't bother to cough. Martin fiddled with the timing, while Pammie said she thought he needed to turn the valve on the fuel line.

"I know what I'm doing, Pammie!" Martin snapped, and again nearly yanked himself out of the boat, to no avail. I called over,

"Do you need any help?"

But by this time Pammie had lost patience. She insisted that she and Martin swap places. I told you she was one of these irritating women who do everything better than you. She switched on the fuel valve, returned the timing settings to their original position, pulled on the starter motor and it immediately roared into life.

"Did you hear Martin swearing?" was the first thing Pammie asked, as she climbed aboard our boat.

"Ian was worse," said Annie.

"I was not," I said. "Was I, Luc?"

I turned to my son and heir for support.

"No," he said. "You were just as bad. But you weren't worse."

Obviously neither Martin nor I were going to get any support. I suggested we retire to the roof for a drink while the women continued with the cooking, and the character assassination.

What happened next, I blame on Rohan's mother, Allanah, who is Annie's younger sister. Allanah, in her youth, belonged to the Perth University and Theatrical Set. As you can imagine there was a great deal of parochialism and not much money in that set. As a result, when Rohan was growing up, her mother and her friends tended to drink local wines like Houghton's White Burgundy, rather than single malt whisky. Forgetting this when Rohan offered to pour the drinks, I assumed she knew that malt whisky was taken in small quantities, cut with a little cool, Highland water. However, this was Australia; it was summer and it was hot, so I agreed when she suggested ice.

"How much scotch, Uncle Ian?" she asked.

"Two fingers."

Rohan nodded, and disappeared with Lucas to prepare the drinks.

When she reappeared on the roof carrying two large tumblers full of pale liquid, and apologising for the glasses because they were the only ones to be had,

I naturally assumed that we were drinking scotch, ice and water. The exertions of the day made us thirsty and we quickly finished our glasses, while we congratulated ourselves on our mutual skill in navigating such badly designed and cumbersome craft. Annie and Pammie joined us for a second drink, and it was only when Rohan appeared for the third time to replenish our glasses that I noticed Martin's voice had become slightly slurred.

"Could you put a bit more water in the scotch this time please, Rohan?" I said.

"Oh!" she said.

Later, I learned the significance of that "Oh". Rohan hadn't put any water at all into the first two drinks. We had been drinking neat scotch. Furthermore, Rohan and Lucas, in consultation, had decided that "two fingers" was a vertical measurement... Still, there was no reason why this should bother us, particularly. The boats were safely moored. The engines were switched off. We weren't going anywhere. But after dinner, the Brookies had to get back to their own houseboat.

Martin was feeling no pain as he climbed into the dinghy and turned to take Baby Eddie from Pammie, who was still standing on the houseboat. He was still feeling no pain when he slipped backwards, fell over and lay on his back like a beached turtle in the bottom of the dinghy, giggling that he couldn't get up.

By this time high tide had passed, and both the tide and the current were now hurtling out to sea together at fifteen knots. I had visions of Baby Eddie going overboard and floating off into the blackness, buoyed up by his little orange life jacket, never to be seen again. I suggested I get into the boat and take the baby from Pammie. Annie reminded me that I had been drinking with Martin. She insisted Pammie get into the dinghy, start the engine, then she would hand the baby to Pammie, and I would get into the dinghy and steer it across to the other houseboat.

"I can start the engine," I said.

Annie just looked at me. I looked at Martin, still lying in the bottom of the dinghy, giggling.

"You start the engine, Pammie," I said.

Getting Eddie off the dinghy at the other end was easy. Pam just picked him up under one arm, grabbed the boat's ladder with the other, and climbed aboard. Willie followed her just as easily, but getting Martin on board was a little more difficult. Eventually, with Pammie pulling and me pushing, we managed it. Then I realised I had a problem. I had to get back to our houseboat and I was in Martin's dinghy.

By now I had sobered up enough to realise that Annie was probably right; I wasn't in any fit state to start the engine on a dinghy without possibly falling over the side. Since the engine was still running in Martin's dinghy, I steered it back to our houseboat, untied our dinghy, towed it across and tethered it to Martin's houseboat, and then returned to ours, still in his dinghy. In other words I swapped dinghies. This was to be very significant, but at the time I didn't give it another thought.

It was a beautiful evening. We were far enough away from civilisation for the stars to appear like a huge, upturned saucer of diamonds, sparkling over the boat and reaching down to the horizon on all sides. Annie and I took a mattress and blankets up onto the roof where we made love and slept. The gentle lapping of the water against the side of the boat lulled us to sleep. It was the only peaceful sleep we were to get for the next week.

CHAPTER TEN
The Race is On.

At home we usually settle for a cup of tea and a piece of toast for breakfast, but the fresh air had given everybody an appetite. Just after dawn, Annie was already back at the stove cooking bacon, eggs, tomatoes, and mushrooms, while I made tea and toast and the kids sat around the table playing UNO. Normally they would have been watching TV but the television worked on the same basis as the ship's radio. Back in the marina, near the Ballina transponder, we had quite a good picture. Away from civilisation, in the lee of the island, the best I could get was a black and white double image of what looked like a snowstorm and sounded like static.

The kids didn't mind. Despite an age range of more than ten years they were going through a stage where they were all mad about playing cards. Uno. Snap. Draw poker. It didn't matter what it was. They would play together for hours. It meant that Annie and I had to do the housekeeping chores, but we didn't mind either. In fact it was pleasant; listening to their chatter and laughter, as the bacon sizzled in the pan, and birds sat in the trees on the bank giving us a sort of dawn chorus.

Suddenly, all that changed. About ten metres away, Martin had started his houseboat engine. The birds flew, startled, into the sky. Kate dropped her Uno cards. The radio crackled into life.

"Rubber Ducky to Big Fish. We're going up to Wardell to get the newspapers. Over."

I picked up the microphone.

"We're having breakfast. We'll meet you there. Over and out."

We expected Martin to move off, the engine noise to subside, and peace to return. It didn't. Martin must have been having trouble raising the anchor because the noise just got louder. I looked out and saw why the noise had got louder. The other houseboat was reversing towards us and was about to smash into our bow. I ran out on deck just in time to lean out over the rail, grab the back rail of Martin's houseboat and hold the two three-tonne monsters apart. I probably wouldn't have succeeded if it hadn't been for our dinghy, which I'd moored to the back of Martin's houseboat the night before. It was now jammed between the two houseboats, holding them apart, and quickly assuming the shape of a banana. I yelled out to tell Martin that he was backing into us. Being in the wheelhouse, of course, he had no view of the back of his boat. Over the roar of the engines, he also had no chance of hearing me. I yelled to Annie to get on the ship's radio, and tell him what was happening. She obviously got through because, although the boat kept moving backwards and the engine continued to whine in neutral, Martin came out on the back deck to investigate.

He looked at me, my feet planted firmly on one boat, hands clamped firmly on the other, trying to prevent the two from turning the dinghy into a sheet of pressed aluminium.

"We're not going backwards," he said.

"You must be!" I said.

"No," he insisted. "You must be coming forwards."

The muscles in my shoulders were beginning to scream with pain. I didn't have time for subtlety.

"You stupid bastard!" I yelled. "We can't be going forward. We haven't got the bloody engine on."

He saw the logic of my finely reasoned argument immediately, disappeared back into the wheelhouse, and put the engine into forward gear.

Slowly the pressure came off my shoulders, and I released the rail of their boat before it dragged me overboard.

Slowly the dinghy trapped between the two houseboats resumed its normal shape. Well, almost. It still seemed a bit bent to me. I decided not to swap dinghies back.

We resumed our breakfast, thinking that Martin would now chug upstream for his newspaper; but he didn't. He must have been having trouble freeing the anchor from the bottom of the river because he kept steering in strange circles, and yelling at Pammie who was operating the electric winch. He was almost alongside us when we heard him yelling to her to:

"Use the winch! Use the winch!"

Pammie insisted she *was* "using the winch" and by way of demonstration pulled on the winch lever to show that the anchor wouldn't shift, no matter what. Frustrated, Martin slammed the houseboat into full forward and the vessel took a terrific lurch as the anchor came free from the bottom. Caught unawares, Pammie was still hanging onto the winch lever as the anchor shot out of the water, slammed against the front rail of the boat, and was catapulted onto the deck with a loud crash. The great chunk of metal missed Pammie by millimetres, but the grey, slimy mud that had held it captive on the riverbed didn't. It spun off the flying anchor and splattered across her face. As the houseboat shot forward under full power, we were just able to hear Pammie yell,

"Next time we weigh anchor, you can handle the winch and I'll handle the wheel!"

Peace returned. Breakfast was served with orange juice for the kids, and a Berocca for me. Lucas and Rohan were anxious for us to get under way but we were in no hurry. It was rather nice being on our own again, so we took our time washing up before I switched on the engine, and upped anchor without incident.

Despite the time at breakfast, we soon caught up with Martin, meandering up the river, taking in the views and the wildlife. He seemed to be in no hurry either, until Willie, on the roof of their houseboat, spotted us, and I swear their houseboat immediately took on pace.

Have you ever been driving along a single-lane

highway in the country when you come across somebody sightseeing? Usually the driver is wearing a hat and wandering along at about sixty kays, oblivious to everything and everybody. You can't overtake because the road is too winding, but then you see a sign that says

"Overtaking Lane Ahead."

Then the driver in front sees the sign too, and immediately slams his foot on the accelerator. Instead of travelling at forty kays below the speed limit, you have to travel at twenty kays above the limit just to keep up with him. Forget about moving out and overtaking.

Then, as soon as the overtaking lane ends, the driver in front slows back to a crawl, and you follow him through the countryside, swearing under your breath.

Well, that's what Martin was like.

As Martin accelerated, Lucas yelled from the roof,

"Catch him, dad."

But every time I accelerated, Martin accelerated, too. In theory, since the houseboats were identical, this should have meant we maintained our relative positions, but for some reason our houseboat was faster than theirs. Probably by no more than half a knot, but when your top speed is about five knots, this is significant.

Gradually we drew alongside Martin, and then edged forward, with both houseboats flat out.

"They're like kids!" Annie called out, as we passed the Brookies.

"Worse!" Pammie called back.

But I didn't care. My houseboat was faster than his.

There was a boat ramp at Wardell, but nowhere to dock the houseboats. We had already anchored midstream, as Martin pulled into Wardell. I ran across in the dinghy, with Lucas and Rohan. As we pulled alongside, I called out,

"Where have you been? We've been here half an hour. We were worried about you."

"Bastard," said Martin, but he was grinning. "Your boat's faster than ours."

"Just a better driver that's all. What were you doing, driving round and round in circles, back at the island?"

"The anchor was stuck," Martin explained. "It's your fault. It's the place you chose to anchor. Too much mud. I'm choosing the anchor spot next time."

"Well, you could," I said. "If you ever got anywhere first."

We took Pammie on board the dinghy, and went

ashore to get the newspapers, fresh milk, and ice creams for the kids.

"You shouldn't encourage him," said Pammie.

"Sorry," I said. "No more racing. Promise."

The kids didn't look pleased, but they needn't have worried; we'd reckoned without Martin. By the time we got back to the houseboats he had already upped anchor and was waiting in the channel with his engine revving, holding the boat's position against the current.

"Thought I'd up anchor while Pammie was away," he said. "Don't want her getting covered in mud again."

His concern fooled nobody. He just wanted to get a flying start. As soon as Pammie was back on board, Martin set off upstream. By the time I got the dinghy back to our boat he was already disappearing under the bridge.

"Where's Martin going?" Annie asked, as we clambered back on board.

"He wants to pick the next mooring spot," I said.

"Well, let him," said Annie.

The kids were disappointed, but I shrugged it off.

"Mum's right," I said. "Let Martin pick the next spot. What harm can it do?"

CHAPTER ELEVEN
Scotch on the Rocks.

Martin was quickly disappearing from view upstream, which meant he was also going out of radio contact. I got onto the radio and asked him where he was going to moor for the night.

"Somewhere where we can fish," came the reply.

I'm not a fisherman. To me "somewhere where we can fish" is in water, and we were already floating on loads of water. I tried to get him to be more specific.

"Are you going past Broadwater? Over."

Broadwater being the next town up river. I think he said yes, but by now he was going around a bend in the river and vision and sound were cut off. We had two options. We could completely ignore him, or we could follow him up river. Since we were heading that way anyway, we decided to follow him.

We were in no hurry. Rohan had never tried fishing,

and we baited a couple of handlines, and tried throwing them overboard. We didn't catch anything and everybody soon got bored.

We decided to move. Everybody disappeared onto the roof as usual and I raised the anchor.

As we motored upstream, we tried trawling a line out the back of the boat, but this was more in hope than expectation.

We stopped to look at Broadwater.

We took a detour into a large inlet that fed into the river, thinking that Martin might have gone in there looking for his "somewhere-to-fish."

The cormorants and pelicans were obviously used to houseboats and ignored us completely. They were obviously better fishermen, too. Cormorants swim almost totally submerged except for their heads and necks and look like miniature prehistoric monsters moving through the water. Occasionally they would dive and disappear, re-emerging with fish in their beaks, which they carried off to some convenient log sticking out of the water. Once there, they appeared to swallow the fish whole before spreading their wings to dry in the sun. The pelicans, on the other hand, just seemed content to sit bobbing on the water doing absolutely nothing, and we were content to steer well clear of any pelicans that didn't bob. We were old hands now; we knew they were standing up.

It was just as well that we had picked up a little rivercraft, because the further upstream we went, the fewer the marker buoys. Past Broadwater, they only seemed to appear at each river bend, so that on the straight stretches we steered a line well to the left of the buoys, and kept a regular lookout from the roof for any tell-tale signs of mudflats. Apart from this, the day was entirely peaceful and relaxing; but as darkness approached and we still hadn't caught up with Martin, we started to get concerned.

Had we missed him? Did we want to find him? Should we go on? Should we just moor before it got dark? Should we turn back to check if we'd passed him without noticing? I was pretty certain we hadn't. A three-tonne steel barge is hard to miss. We'd kept the radio on all the way. Even if we'd missed him, surely he would have spotted us passing and called us.

As it got dark, I was beginning to think Martin had simply kept going into the night and that we should stop looking; but as we rounded the next bend in the river, there was the Brookies houseboat, moored near the northern bank by an idyllic, wide, flat meadow. The shore here was actually sandy. The water was blue. I thought it looked a bit exposed. I preferred mooring in the lee of a high bank and trees, but Annie pointed out to me that I knew no more about choosing a place to moor than Martin did, so I shrugged, and manoeuvred the boat downstream of Martin's to drop anchor.

Everybody was on the roof again, which meant they missed the brilliance of my docking manoeuvre. I turned the boat upstream, dropped the anchor, leaned through the window and pushed the engine into neutral. The boat started to drift back, the anchor caught, and we stopped, bobbing on the waves like a giant pelican; a bit out of proportion, but with a certain charm.

"That was easy..??" said Annie, climbing down from the roof.

"Well, you get used to it," I said modestly, securing the anchor line. Almost immediately, a man in a kayak appeared alongside the houseboat. I have no idea where he came from.

"Ahoy," he called. "I suppose you know you're moored on an outcrop of rocks, do you?"

Stupid question really. Of course we didn't.

"Will we be stranded here?" I asked.

"Oh no," he said. "But at low tide, you won't be able to move."

What were we to do? We were already moored. Whether we moved now or later when the tide was fully in, didn't seem to matter. We decided to take the dinghy across to Martin's houseboat to discuss our options. We were having dinner there anyway.

As soon as we pulled the dinghy alongside their houseboat and I stepped aboard, Will was standing there, staring up at me and looking rather nervous.

"I'm sorry, Uncle Ian," he said.

Thinking he was talking about the mooring spot, I tousled his hair and smiled.

"That's okay, Willie," I said. "It's not your fault."

"Yes it is," said Martin. "Tell Uncle Ian what you did, Willie."

"I lost your fishing rod," said Will.

"I told Willie you'd be angry, Uncle Ian," said Martin.

I wasn't angry. I was totally confused. I've never owned a fishing rod in my life.

Martin explained. The truth is that Martin wasn't any

more of a fisherman than me, but since marrying Pammie and becoming part of her sports-mad family, he had been forced to assume a sportsmanlike manner to impress the in-laws. This included heading up to the mountains in summer with Mick, Pammie's intrepid father, to go fly fishing; as well as heading up to the mountains in winter, where he had already broken his nose learning to ski. Having thus ingratiated himself with his father-in-law, Martin had borrowed a couple of very sophisticated rods from him for the trip. After he'd moored, he'd decided to set up both the rods so that I could join him fishing at dusk, which apparently is the time to fish. He had already prepared one rod, and was working on the second when Will asked if he could try fishing.

"Sure," said Martin, and fixed some bait onto the first rod, before returning to assemble the second.

You have to remember that Will was just three years old at the time. He stood there, holding the rod, which was at least three times as tall as he was, wondering what to do next.

"What do I do?" he asked, quite reasonably.

"Just cast it over the side," said Martin, without looking up.

"What does 'cast' mean?"

"Throw it. Just throw it," said Martin.

Will looked at his father's bowed head. Had he heard right? He was sure he had. He threw the rod over the side. Not just the hook and the line; the whole rod.

Martin looked up when he heard the splash in the water. He rushed to the side of the boat.

The rod was already being carried off by the current, and fast disappearing under the water.

Martin turned to Willie, horrified.

"What have you done?" he asked.

"You said throw it," said Will.

"Uncle Ian's going to be very angry with you," said Martin. "That was his rod."

On hearing the story, I hid my disappointment as best I could. I told Willie it just meant I couldn't go fishing with his Dad today; he'd have to go on his own. But Daddy would have to buy me another rod when we got back to Melbourne.

"I will too," Martin said in a low voice. "That was Mick's favourite rod. He didn't want to lend it to me. He'll kill me if he finds out I've lost it."

It seemed to me that we had more pressing problems;

the rocks below us. Should we move? Annie and Pammie decided there was no point. It was dark already. We couldn't see any rocks, and we were as likely to run into them as over them. Besides, the tide was coming in; we'd be safe until the morning.

We were safe until the morning; until about four in the morning, when I was woken by a bang and a shudder. Either we had been hit by Martin's houseboat or we had hit the rocks. I got up and looked across the water.

Martin's houseboat was still at a safe distance but Martin was peering over the side into the water.

"I think we were hit by a floating log," he called out.

"I think we've run aground," I yelled back.

We were both wrong, but I was less wrong than he was.

As the sun came up we could see a row of jagged rocks running along the length of the houseboats on the southern side. We were actually in a channel running between the rocks and the shore. Still afloat, but every time the houseboat moved on its anchor we nudged into the rocks, and swung back.

Now I knew why the houseboats were made of three tonnes of steel. Apart from losing a few coats of paint, the rocks had no effect at all, other than to keep the houseboats captive until the tide came back in. There was nothing for us to do but wait. While I ferried Kate and Willie ashore so they could run wild in the meadow, Rohan and Lucas returned to their ongoing card game, and Martin manoeuvred his dinghy out through the rocks, and went fishing off the edge of the reef. We were all set for a lazy day, at least until the tide turned.

CHAPTER TWELVE
"The Compleat Angler."

Annie, Pammie, and I sat on the roof of our houseboat where we could keep an eye on Will and Kate in the meadow. The roof was surrounded by a safety rail, the gaps between the rails covered in chicken wire. By putting a chair across the top of the ladder connecting with the lower deck, we formed a safe playpen for Baby Eddie, and a comfortable place to sunbathe for ourselves.

We were planning to build a house on the farm and we spent the time discussing various floorplans. Annie had been reading Enid Blyton's *The Faraway Tree* to Kate, and was keen that we too should have a Slippery-Slip, running from the top of the house to the bottom. I reminded her that the Faraway Tree also had a basket on a rope, so that the cushions the kids slid down on could be pulled back up. Since a basket on a rope seemed a bit impractical in a house, I envisaged spending the rest of my life carrying

"The Compleat Angler"

pillows and cushions back upstairs. I suggested a fireman's pole. Pammie thought somebody would probably stagger into the hole surrounding the pole in the middle of the night, and break their neck. She suggested a laundry shute. Then we remembered that to take advantage of the view, we were going to have the living quarters upstairs and the bedrooms downstairs, which meant clothes wouldn't be discarded upstairs, and having a laundry shute would be rather pointless. In the end we decided we'd have to settle for a staircase.

Annie had some graph paper and drew up a rough sketch to show the architect. It was a good plan, a central kitchen, dining, and living area, with bedrooms running off into two separate wings, so that the two families could have some privacy. While Annie did the drawing, Pammie entertained Eddie, and I watched Martin fishing.

I thought fishing was supposed to be relaxing, but the way Martin tackled it, it was more like an Olympic endurance event. As soon as he had reached a point on the reef, he dropped anchor, switched off the engine, threw burley onto the water to attract the fish, baited his hook, and cast overboard. He would cast slightly upstream of the boat, and the line would immediately float back down towards the boat with Martin reeling the line in as it approached. The hook was in the water for such a short time that the fish needed to be world class sprinters to even catch the hook, let alone take the bait.

The other problem was the burley. Like Martin's line, it too was carried away on the current; so that while he fruitlessly cast and reeled in, downstream, the local fish were all having a feast. I suspect that they were also having a great time teasing Martin. Because no matter where he anchored, the fish would start leaping out of the water a few yards further along the reef, and Martin would soon become convinced he was in the wrong spot, up anchor and repeat the whole process again somewhere else.

Actually, he wouldn't always repeat the process. In fact, most of the time he would reel in, up anchor, try to restart the engine, fail, and then drift down past the houseboats until Pammie or I would have to get into the second dinghy and go and rescue him. The first time he relocated, Martin did try restarting the outboard while he was still anchored; but he soon realised that while he was safely moored, we would just leave him there to keep on trying. That's when he settled on the idea of up-anchoring first, so that if the engine didn't start we would have to rescue him. Even then, Pammie would leave it to the last minute.

"He's adrift again," I would say.

"Wait till he drifts down to us," Pammie would say. "It won't be as far to go to fetch him."

Each time we let Martin drift further and further before we rescued him, and he'd be standing in the boat, hand on hip, yelling,

"Well, is somebody going to get me?"

As I towed him back up to his fishing spot for the umpteenth time, Martin was bemoaning the fact that he never had any luck. How come his outboard wouldn't start and mine would? I suggested that perhaps it had been damaged while being crushed between the two houseboats on the first morning. He suggested that we should swap dinghies but I pointed out to him that if we did and he got stranded again, I wouldn't be able to rescue him.

Annie made things worse. Each time Pammie or I towed Martin back, she would call out,

"Have you caught anything Martin?"

He never had. He claimed that all he caught were

catfish that he threw back in, but the only thing I saw him catch on the whole trip was Luc's foot, when Luc accidentally stepped on a hook that had been dropped on the deck. Fortunately Pammie was there to cauterise Martin's fishing knife and cut the hook out of Luc's foot, because we couldn't pull it out against the barbs. I let Pammie do this because she is an *Orthodontist*. I knew she wouldn't faint at the sight of Luc's blood.

When Luc was five, he'd ridden his bicycle into a lemon tree on Lord Howe island and badly gashed his face and throat on its inch-long thorns. Medical facilities on the island were not exactly sophisticated. They'd had to get the doctor out of the golf club where he had been propping up the bar for a few hours. His hands were shaking, and at first I refused to let him touch Luc, but then he disappeared into his surgery and re-emerged after obviously having taken something because his hands were now relatively steady. I had to hold Luc in my arms while the doctor, using only a local anaesthetic, put ten stitches in Luc's cheek and six in his throat. Lucas was very brave. In fact I cried more than he did, as the doctor stitched away, and Annie told Luc stories from "The Lion the Witch and the Wardrobe", trying to distract him.

"The Compleat Angler"

After that, I couldn't face the prospect of cutting into Luc's flesh to remove anything, even something as small as a fishhook.

The sun was getting quite high and it was getting hot on the roof of the houseboat when, once again, the silence was broken by the sound of Martin yanking on the starting motor. It obviously wasn't going to start, and we waited until he drifted down towards us, but this time he didn't seem to be getting any nearer. In fact he seemed to be drifting further away. His shouts seemed to be getting quieter and quieter, too. I looked over the side of the houseboat. The tide had turned and now ran up river. The water level was also rising, and the rocks alongside the houseboat were beginning to disappear beneath the waves. We'd soon be able to move.

I contemplated collecting Willie and Kate from the meadow first so that I could start our houseboat and be ready to leave as soon as we rescued Martin. That way we could be sure of reaching our next mooring spot first, and not spend the next day marooned on rocks. Then I remembered that our boat was faster than Martin's, so I climbed into the dinghy and set off to save him yet again.

We couldn't have left the reef any earlier, anyway.

Big Fish to Rubber Ducky

Even with the incoming tide we had to avoid rocks still lurking just beneath the surface. How we'd both moored the previous night without running aground seemed to be some sort of a miracle, but if we'd got in without incident, we could get out the same way. Martin and I took the dinghy and plotted a course out of the reef to deep water with a plumb line from our houseboat.

A plumb line is just a piece of rope with a weight on the end, which you drop overboard to test the water's depth. When the weight stops dropping, you've touched the bottom. We thus carefully manoeuvred the houseboats out into safe water. Everything was done in slow motion, with Luc dropping the plumb line over the side of the houseboat as we edged out, to make sure we were keeping to the safe channel.

We waited until Martin was also into safe water, then I put the engine into full forward, and the houseboat surged ahead. Annie winced at the roar of the motor.

"Slow down," she said.

"Do you want Martin to choose the next mooring spot?" I asked.

We moved on, the silence only broken by the whine of the engine.

CHAPTER THIRTEEN
It's Only a Game.

Having lost most of the day stuck on the rocks, we had little time to explore further upstream. We had agreed to meet the manager on the farm in two days time, so we would soon have to head back to Ballina. About mid-afternoon I found a perfect spot. On a wide sweep of the river, the River Gums came right to the water's edge but the bank dropped sharply thereafter, giving us plenty of depth. I decided to avoid another night swinging on the anchor by tying the back of the houseboat to a tree, and dropping the anchor from the front to stop us swinging into the bank instead. Of course, this meant we didn't have to drop anchor before switching off the engine, so for the first and only time, Lucas and Rohan were allowed to help moor the boat by jumping ashore and tying off the rope.

Big Fish to Rubber Ducky

We were on the southern bank, facing west; we could watch the sunset, but the high bank and trees would shade us from the sunrise. With any luck we'd be able to sleep in until at least six thirty. The restless night on the rocks had left me a bit tired.

Martin, of course, wasn't going to moor alongside us. I think it was a matter of pride. He didn't want to admit that he had chosen badly the previous night or that I'd chosen well tonight. Instead, he moored out in the stream where he seemed to be laying out yards and yards of anchor chain before he eventually switched off the engine, and Pammie drove him and the kids across to our houseboat in the dinghy. As he clambered aboard, I asked him why he had laid out so long an anchor.

"The anchor wouldn't hold, Bradders," he said. "It's too deep here, and there's too much mud."

"You prefer shallow with lots of rocks, do you Martin?" I asked.

He insisted the mooring place the previous night had been fine; we'd all been safe, hadn't we? I reminded him we'd also been marooned for the better part of a day.

Annie cut in, saying that since we were arguing anyway, why didn't we all play Monopoly after dinner?

It's Only a Game

The kids had been asking to play. Everybody was keen; everybody but me. I knew how the game would end.

Monopoly is supposed to be a game of high finance so you'd think we adults would have an advantage. You'd be wrong. All the kids, but especially Luc, have a very healthy, competitive spirit, so that while we were chatting and refilling our wine glasses, Luc would be landing on our properties, and moving on again without paying rent before we noticed anything. Eventually Martin would cotton on to this.

"Hang on," he'd say. "Fenchurch Street Station. That's mine. You owe me twenty dollars."

"Too late," Lucas would say. "You've already thrown the dice."

After that, at every throw of the dice, Martin would check if anybody had landed on his property. If it wasn't his property, he'd then go all around the table until he found out who did own the property. I'd get fed up with the delays and tell him to hurry up. We'd all have another drink, and in the meantime Lucas would have bought up half the board and put hotels on Mayfair and Park Lane. From then on it was just a matter of time, really.

Sooner or later Martin would land on Mayfair, and couldn't pay.

He'd offer Luc Fenchurch Street Station and Euston Street for fifteen hundred dollars, and Luc would accept.

I'd point out to Luc that they weren't worth that much.

Annie would tell me to leave Luc alone. He knew what he was doing.

I would point out that Luc was only nine.

Martin would point out that Luc was, really, nearly ten.

And Luc would point out that if he didn't accept Martin's offer, Martin would be out, and the game would be over.

I would point out that this was the whole purpose of the game. This is how you win.

Luc would point out that since he owned all the property now and was going to win anyway, he might as well enjoy prolonging the agony for everyone else.

Checkmate.

The game on the houseboat that night followed the familiar path. I was only saved by the sight of Martin's houseboat suddenly floating past us in the dark, narrowly missing our anchor chain. We went to investigate.

The tide had turned yet again, and it wasn't clear whether their houseboat was just swinging on the very long anchor chain or whether the anchor was dragging along the bottom, and the boat was adrift. I again suggested that Martin tie up to a tree but he refused. He said he wasn't having any possums climbing aboard along the rope, and biting his toe. Instead, he took his family back to his houseboat where he spent the entire night wandering around, still trying to decide whether the boat was drifting or just swinging on its anchor.

The reference to the possum was an old family joke which dates back to our first trip in a houseboat, on the Myall Lakes. The Myall Lakes are land-locked lakes, separated from the sea only by sand dunes. As a result, the lakes are tidal because the sea filters through the sand, but because the water is filtered, they are tidal freshwater lakes. The water is crystal clear, and even in the deepest parts the sand on the bottom is visible from the surface. Not much good for scuba diving because hardly anything lives on the sandy bottom, but great for house boating and swimming. The only drawback is that the houseboats are hired from Bulahdelah, about ten miles up the Myall River, on the Pacific Highway, north of Newcastle.

Big Fish to Rubber Ducky

To get to the lakes you have to navigate the river for a couple of hours. The first time you do it, it can take even longer.

The river is quite narrow and twisting, and the steerage on a houseboat is not like a car's. When you turn the wheel it has no immediate effect. For some time you continue on in a straight line, until the rudder eventually starts to turn the boat. This takes some getting used to. There is a tendency to panic. You turn the wheel. Nothing happens. You turn the wheel again. By this time the effect of the first turn is just kicking in, and instead of making a slight adjustment in direction, you find yourself heading straight for the bank. You quickly spin the steering wheel the other way. Again nothing happens. Then, after bouncing off the bank, protected only by the rubber tyres that hang around the perimeter of the houseboat for this very reason, you head back into the centre of the river. But, once more, you've over-compensated, and now you are heading for the other bank to repeat the process.

After an hour or more of zig-zagging down the river, bumping into the bank and narrowly avoiding the trees that grow in the shallows, you get used to the steering just in time to glide effortlessly into to a little lagoon which separates the river mouth from the lakes. You aren't going to venture onto the lake in the dark, so you moor in the lagoon. In our case, we tied off to a tree near a picnic area on the bank and settled down to champagne, chicken, and salad. Lucas was only a toddler; Kate wasn't yet born, and Martin and Pammie weren't with us. Instead, a couple called Maura and Charles made up the party. Actually they weren't a couple; but Charles was teaching me to scuba dive, and Maura had once travelled to Asia with us, when Luc was about five months old, so we all knew each other well.

That is, we knew each other well in the city. This was our first experience together in the wild, so to speak. We were all sitting on the aft deck having supper when Maura suddenly let out a shriek and ran into the cabin, turning at the door to stare back into the darkness in terror. Annie and Charles looked to see what had frightened Maura. Then they both made a dash for the cabin too, leaving three-year-old Luc and me to face the danger alone. The danger was a ring-tailed possum, which had ventured on to the mooring line and was sitting there watching us intently, with large luminous eyes.

I couldn't believe three adults could be afraid of such a delightful little creature.

"It's probably hungry, Luc," I said.

I took a piece of cucumber from the remains of the salad, and offered it to the possum. It was obviously used to being fed at the picnic area because it took the cucumber, then it took the carrot, the green peppers, and everything else that I could find left in the salad bowl. At first, probably as much from my nervousness as anything, it dropped a couple of pieces, but soon we had a good routine going. I would hold the piece of vegetable out. The possum would take it in its teeth, then transfer it to its paws, to chew pieces off.

Luc was enchanted. Not enchanted enough to actually feed the possum himself but that was mainly because the other three adults were setting him a bad example by being such wimps. I told them so. I shouldn't have been so cocky.

When the possum had eaten all the salad in the bowl, he jumped lightly onto the deck, and started foraging around for the small scraps he had dropped. I was barefoot and unfortunately, in the poor light, my big toe must have looked like a piece of onion or maybe apple.

Whatever it looked like, the possum took a good bite at it. I let out a yell. Terrified, the possum shot back up along the rope onto the shore and disappeared. The three adults in the cabin collapsed into hysterical giggles. Only Luc was at all sympathetic as I washed the blood off my toe under the shower, and complained that it was no laughing matter. I might have got tetanus or rabies or something. I don't know why Annie keeps telling people this story.

There seemed to be no possums in the trees on the Richmond River, and we would have spent a peaceful night if it weren't for Martin wandering around on his boat, peering overboard, and trying to gauge whether he was adrift. I slept fitfully, occasionally wakening when Martin's houseboat swung particularly close. Finally, Annie woke up with a scream. She was having a nightmare. She was sure the trees from the bank were crashing in on us. I assured her we were quite safe.

"Well, something moved," she insisted.

I told her it was Martin, and we both got up, made a cup of tea, and leaned on the boat rail watching Martin stomping around the deck of his boat like Captain Ahab on a stormy night at sea.

Big Fish to Rubber Ducky

"I don't think I can stand another three nights like this, Ian," said Annie. "Do you think next time we could persuade Martin to moor further away?"

I decided I'd speak to him in the morning.

CHAPTER FOURTEEN
Round One...

If I had slept better on the previous two nights, I might have phrased it differently. Instead I said,

"What the hell were you doing clumping about on deck all night, Martin?"

He assumed his usual look of vague innocence.

"I couldn't sleep."

"Well at least you could have stayed below deck so the rest of us could sleep," I said.

"Then he'd have kept the baby awake," said Pammie.

"I tell you what," I said to Pammie, "You bring Willie and the baby to sleep on our houseboat tonight, and we'll let Martin moor on his own, as far away from all of us as possible."

"I don't know what you're picking on me for," said Martin. "I haven't done anything."

"You haven't done anything! You practically squashed the dinghy. You practically rammed your houseboat into ours. You practically decapitated Pammie with the anchor. You marooned us on a load of rocks. We spend half our time coming out in the dinghy to rescue you. You spend the entire night doing pirouettes on the end of the anchor chain and giving Annie nightmares, and you reckon you haven't done anything? You shouldn't oughta be let out in charge of a houseboat!" I said.

"I'm just as good a skipper as you," Martin said. "If your engine wasn't faster than mine, I'd have found much better mooring spots."

I snorted in derision. I told Martin he couldn't beat me to anywhere, even with half an hour's start. It was all very mature.

"Alright," he said. "Give me a half-hour's start and I'll race you back to Ballina."

"We're not due on the farm until tomorrow," said Pammie. "I'm not spending the night tied up at the marina."

"At least we might get a decent night's sleep," I said, but she was adamant.

In the end we agreed to race back to the island at

which we had stopped on the first night, and moor there, before heading for Ballina in the morning.

As I returned to our houseboat in the dinghy, Martin was already switching on the engine and starting to pull in the anchor. I saw Willie disappearing up onto the roof, followed by Pammie, carrying the baby. I guessed Pammie and Annie must have been talking.

I climbed back on board our houseboat.

"What's happening?" asked Annie.

"We're racing back to the island," I said.

Luc immediately jumped ashore to release the mooring line.

"How is that going to help us get a decent night's sleep?" Annie asked.

"I'm not sure," I said. "But at least we know we'll be mooring somewhere safe."

But I'd reckoned without the constantly changing nature of the river.

As Martin approached the next bend downriver, I started the engine. He was obviously watching me because he immediately came on the radio.

"Rubber Ducky to Big Fish. Half an hour's start, remember. Over."

Big Fish to Rubber Ducky

"Big Fish to Rubber Ducky. I'm still on the anchor. Over," I replied, but I am not sure he heard me because he didn't answer.

"I'm not waiting here half an hour with the engine revving," said Annie.

"Neither am I," I said, as soon as Martin was out of sight. "Let's get the anchor up."

There was an immediate scramble for the ladder onto the roof, and I was left to raise the anchor alone, with Luc and Rohan yelling from the roof for me to hurry up.

I was pretty confident I could catch Martin but the distance to the first bend was further than I thought, and for a long time we lost sight of him completely. Luc and Rohan kept watch from the roof and Annie went back to bed where she stayed, asleep, until we reached Wardell. From Wardell to Ballina the river runs almost straight northeast, and when the tide is coming in, as it was now, the water rushes through the narrows near the bridge. When the wind blows a gale from the northeast the waves on the river actually have whitecaps. Add to this the fact that the gale was bringing driving rain, and you'll appreciate that conditions were pretty difficult. By now we were fairly close to Martin but I couldn't overtake him in the narrows. Once through the bridge, I tried to move up on his left-hand side. He moved his houseboat to the left. I pulled back, tried going up the right hand side. He let his boat ease to the right. It was like Damon Hill and Michael Schumacher, only in slow motion, with driving rain and three-foot-high waves. To make matters worse the wind, waves, and rain made it difficult to see the marker buoys.

Suddenly Annie was at my elbow.

"What are you doing?" she asked.

"I'm trying to overtake Martin," I said.

"You're trying to kill us," she said. "Mooring at that island in this weather is going to be hard enough without the two of you fighting to get in first."

"We won't be able to moor in the same place, anyway," I said. "The wind's in the wrong direction."

And then it struck me. On the first night, we'd moored on the easterly side of the island because the wind was coming from the southwest. Today, we ought to moor on the westerly side because the wind was coming from the opposite direction. I eased back on the engine, and steered left while Martin ploughed on into the rising waves.

As soon as we came into the lee of the island, the wind dropped, the river flattened, and the rain stopped beating against the side of the boat.

"What are you doing now?" asked Annie.

"Mooring in the lee of the island, out of the wind," I said.

"Aren't you going to tell Martin?" she asked.

"No"

Annie tutted, picked up the microphone, and called over the radio.

"Big Fish to Rubber Ducky. Over."

No reply.

"The island's blocking the radio waves," I said.

Annie hung up the radio.

"You're worse than the kids," she said.

I just smiled.

When we were safely moored, and Annie still hadn't managed to raise Martin on the radio, she insisted that I take the dinghy and go around the island and find them. She also insisted that the kids couldn't come with me because it would be dangerous out in the wind. I was beginning to think I carried too much life insurance.

Actually it wasn't as bad as I thought. I went around

the north side of the island keeping as close as possible to the shore to get some relief from the wind. I found Martin moored pretty much where we had been the first night. The boat was rocking quite dramatically on the anchor line, which slackened and tightened every time a wave hit the side. Pammie was looking anxiously over the side as I approached.

"Where have you been?" she asked as I drew alongside. "We've been here nearly half an hour. We were worried about you."

This time she wasn't joking.

"We're moored on the other side of the island," I said. "Out of the wind."

Pammie turned to Martin.

"I told you," she said.

Martin looked at me.

"You said the race was to here."

I shrugged.

"It's no good mooring here in this wind, is it, Martin?"

"We'll move," he said. "But I won the race."

"You're worse than the kids," said Pammie.

I was right. Pammie and Annie *had* been talking.

CHAPTER FIFTEEN
No More Races!

Martin brought his houseboat around to the lee of the island, and under instruction from Pammie who was in contact with Annie on the radio, he moored a respectable distance away from us. He also moored on a shorter anchor. When he eventually switched off the engine and Lucas, Rohan, and I had stopped clapping, Pammie yelled across the water.

"No more racing. Right, Annie?"

"Right." Annie yelled back.

Women. They can take the fun out of anything.

Martin shrugged and started preparing his fishing gear for another attack on the fish. I decided I might as well catch up on some sleep. Rohan and Luc were bored, and hot. The rain had stopped and the air was heavy and humid. They decided they'd like to go swimming. I thought it was too dangerous, because of the current.

Katie was convinced there were sharks in the water. Despite this, Annie decided she'd go over the side herself, and see if it was safe.

She slid off the front of the boat, surfaced, and immediately started swimming furiously as she moved quickly past the boat. The problem was she was swimming in one direction and travelling in the opposite direction. The current was sweeping her away. It was like a gag in some old silent movie.

I ran to the back and threw a rope over the side. She grabbed onto it, and I started to pull her to the side of the boat. Pulling against the current was difficult. Pulling her out of the water was impossible. Martin was very helpful. Across the water I could hear him calling to Pammie.

"Quick, Pammie. Get the camera! Get the camera!"

I was too busy holding on to the rope to notice whether Martin ever did get the camera, but Annie was always convinced he had. Even at the time, exhausted, and panting, as she struggled to get out of the water, she managed to find enough breath to hiss through clenched teeth:

"If the bastard shoots this, I'll kill him!"

The more immediate problem was preventing the current from killing Annie.

Kate was hysterical. She kept yelling,

"Get out of the water, mummy! There's sharks! Sharks!"

Which was about as helpful as Martin's call for the camera.

Eventually, with the help of the older kids, I managed to tie the rope off on the rail so I didn't need to hang on to it. Then by lying flat on my stomach I reached down and grabbed Annie's arm with one hand, her leg with the other, and hauled her out of the water. She clung to the side of the rail for a moment, to get her breath back, then got back on board and comforted Kate who was crying and telling Annie she shouldn't swim with the sharks.

Pammie called from the other boat, asking if Annie was all right. I told her Annie was fine, apart from a few cuts and abrasions on her legs, where she'd dragged up against the boat.

"I'll get the first aid kit," said Pammie, and she, Martin, and the kids came across in the dinghy. By the time they pulled alongside, both Kate and Annie had regained their composure.

Annie glowered down at Martin.

"You didn't film that, did you, Martin?"

Martin grinned, and tried to look innocent.

"No," he said. "Course not."

"Show me the camera," said Annie.

"I haven't got it," said Martin. "I think I'll go fishing."

And after dropping Pammie and the kids off on our houseboat he gunned the outboard, and headed upstream to fish off the edge of the mud flats. Annie is convinced to this day that Martin recorded the whole incident but if he did, he has never admitted it, which is very wise of him.

After that, life pretty much returned to normal. The older kids played cards, Pammie looked after the baby, Annie prepared lunch, and I waited for the inevitable moment when Martin's outboard would fail to start and I'd have to go and rescue him.

"Let him go," said Annie, as his dinghy drifted past us.

Even if he hadn't filmed the incident, Annie wasn't going to easily forgive him for calling for the camera in the first place. We let Martin drift down past his own houseboat before I went to retrieve him. This time, when we pulled his dinghy alongside, nobody, not even

Pammie, could get his outboard to start again. It seemed to have seized up solid.

"You'll just have to fish off the side of the houseboat," said Pammie.

"You can't catch fish off a houseboat!" said Martin.

"You can't catch fish, anywhere," said Pammie. "Besides, it's about time you took your turn looking after the kids, instead of wasting your time fishing."

Martin was quite hurt, but Pammie was right. The kids had been confined to the boat for a couple of days now, and were beginning to go stir crazy. They needed some exercise.

When I'd taken the dinghy around to the other side of the island to find Pammie, I'd noticed a small sandy beach on a bend in the river. I suggested we ferry everyone across there in our dinghy. The kids could make sandcastles, and we could all stretch our legs. As we were now a dinghy down, it took a couple of trips to get everybody to the beach, but it seemed worth the effort. The beach was completely secluded, and protected by a high bank, on top of which stood a tall crop that looked like it might be maize. There wasn't a soul to be seen. In fact we hadn't seen anybody other than our own families since the kayaker had appeared, to tell us we were marooned, three days earlier.

The kids were already making sandcastles as I ferried Martin ashore with his ubiquitous fishing rod. No sooner had we stepped onto the sand than a farmer appeared at the top of the bank, staring down at us.

"You know you're trespassing, do you?" he asked.

I wondered if everybody on the river spoke in rhetorical questions, and was about to argue that the land between high and low tide was, in fact, Crown land, and therefore we (the public) could use it without hindrance; but before I could reply, he noticed the baby. His attitude changed completely. He smiled. He made "goo goo" noises at the baby. He told us he had a grandson in Sydney just about the same age. He told us he thought we were those bloody skiers who came up the river making a racket and causing erosion to the banks. He told us that of course we could let the kids play on the beach. He told us not to let them into the water, though. This was a breeding ground for sharks.

Katie had insisted there were sharks in the water ever since the older kids had first decided they wanted to go swimming. Annie thought she was psychic.

I said I didn't believe it. For a start, there was nothing for the sharks to eat; there were no fish. Martin had been fishing the area for days, and had caught nothing.

"Oh there are lots of fish here," said our new friend the Farmer. "I catch lots of flathead and bream from the bank just up there."

He pointed along the bank in the general direction of where Martin had been mooring his dinghy.

"Do you think I could fish from there?" asked Martin.

"Sure, go ahead," said the Farmer. "You're bound to catch something."

He was wrong. Martin sat for hours on the bank and caught nothing, while the kids played in the sand.

When we decided it was time to return to the houseboat for dinner, Martin sat for hours fishing off the side of the houseboat.

When I got up to go to the bathroom during the night, I swear I saw his silhouette hunched at the rails of his houseboat, still fishing.

He denied it, of course, but certainly when we all got up at dawn, there he was.

Years later, we spent Christmas up at the farm with Stan Walsh and his family and we hired a Bar-B-Q boat to sail up the river to the island, and have lunch. While I was grilling the steaks, Luc threw a handline over the side and almost immediately caught a bream. Sherri, Stan's wife, who is good at these things, gutted and scaled the fish and we cooked it on the barbecue. It was delicious. It was also the only fish I ever saw caught on that river.

CHAPTER SIXTEEN
Back to the Land.

Martin had become so obsessed with the idea that he had to catch at least one fish, that he even lost interest in racing. As we upped anchor and cruised past their houseboat on the way back to the marina, Martin was still fishing, and Pammie was telling him to pack up his gear and get the houseboat engine started.

"Alright. Alright," Martin said, reluctantly reeling in his line. "There's no hurry. It's not a race."

In fact this was the only day when there was a hurry because we'd arranged to meet Berry Spooner, our farm consultant. Berry was a pioneer of the Macadamia industry, and responsible for the establishment of our farm and its conversion from a weed-infested cow paddock into a picture-perfect nut farm. To me Berry was the quintessential country Australian: friendly, laconic, and a lot sharper than he first appeared, so I was surprised to hear that he originally came from Sydney. He even had that characteristic habit shared by so many bushmen who wear hats. When he was confused or puzzled, he would push his hat back on his head and scratch his head while still holding the hat in place between his thumb and forefinger. He'd then pull his hat back onto his head before speaking. Whenever he made this gesture he reminded me of Athol Pacey, an old guy from Ballarat with whom we'd shared another fateful adventure with Martin and Pammie.

We were all partners in a racehorse once, called *Mandapine*. Annie said the name reminded her of a toilet cleaner, and certainly the money we wasted on the filly could just as well have been put down the toilet. She did show some promise as an unraced two-year-old, and on her first visit to the racetrack for a Seymour Maiden, we decided to back her.

The problem was, being unraced, the bookies would be on their guard, so it was important we all got our money on at once. The five of us, Martin, Pammie, Athol, Annie, and I decided we'd take a separate portion of the ring each, and move in simultaneously to place our bets when the price was at its longest. We also decided we needed a signal so we could all move together; a signal that wouldn't alert the bookmakers and cause them to turn their prices down.

Athol habitually wore a flat cap, and we agreed that he would give the signal. As he moved in to back the horse, he'd push his cap back onto the back of his head, scratch his head, pull his cap back into place. On that signal, we'd all move in.

We took our places around the ring, and Athol wandered down to the bookies furthest away from us so that we wouldn't all be rushing the same bookmaker. But he walked too far. At one end of the ring they were betting on the local horses; at the other, they were betting on the Sydney races.

Athol wandered into the Sydney ring by mistake, looked up at the betting boards to see what price they were betting *Mandapine*, couldn't see the horse's name, and became confused. Of course, when he became confused, he always pushed his cap back on his head, scratched his head, and pulled his cap forward again.

This was the signal. Immediately, Pammie, Martin, Annie, and I rushed in and secured ten to one from four different bookies. Realising the plunge was on, everybody started backing *Mandapine* and her price tumbled. Athol came running back through the ring.

"I missed the price," he said. "Somebody's backed it."

We told him,

"We backed it. You gave the signal."

"No, I didn't," he said. "I couldn't even see the horse's name on the board."

We decided to share our bets with Athol which meant that he too, got ten to one, and he too, lost his money when the horse missed the kick and flashed home to run fourth. As a result, the next time she ran, she was favourite; but although she jumped on terms, she just didn't show the zest we knew she had, and again was narrowly beaten. On this second occasion, the five of us went around to the stalls to discuss why we had, once more, lost our money.

Mandapine was standing headfirst in the stall with her bum sticking out, and the trainer peering up her backside.

"What went wrong?" I asked.

"The jockey said she was making a noise," said the Trainer. "Wind."

"Wind," I said knowledgeably. "She's got a breathing problem?"

"No," he said. "Wind in the vagina."

We all stood around, looking up the horse's bum, wondering what the hell he was talking about.

"Can you do anything for that?" asked Martin.

"Yes," said the Trainer. "We can sew up the vagina."

I looked across at Pammie in time to see her wince. In fact I think I winced myself. In the end we got into a huddle and decided that sewing up a horse's vagina was a big price to pay for winning a few bucks on a horse race, so we gave up our lease on the horse, and retired from racing.

I don't think Berry ever owned a racehorse. He was much too level-headed. The only crazy thing he ever seemed to do was drive us up and down the farm's more precipitous slopes in his four wheel drive when we did our periodic tours of inspection. In the early days, before the trees were established and the grass had given the slopes a secure surface, we would often go sliding sideways down the hill with Berry wrestling with the wheel, and the rest of us hanging on for dear life. We were due for another tour of inspection that day but first we had to return Martin's disabled dinghy to the marina for repair.

We arrived at the marina first but the quayside was occupied with other boats so we had to tie up to a buoy on the other side of the river. After we'd tied up, I took Annie and the kids ashore, went back, ferried Pammie and the kids ashore, then went back again to tow Martin and his dinghy across. About ten yards from the marina, my outboard died as well. The Deckhand came out to tow us both in. He took a quick look at my outboard.

"Have you put any petrol in it?" he asked.

"No," I said.

"It's out of petrol."

While the Deckhand refilled my outboard motor, and inspected Martin's outboard, Martin kept saying,

"Fancy forgetting to put petrol in it, Bradders. Fancy forgetting to put petrol in it."

I thought he was chancing his luck, particularly when the Deckhand announced that *his* engine had completely seized up. It seemed to be knocked out of shape, the Deckhand said. As if somebody had given it a hefty whack?

I looked at Martin.

"Well I haven't hit it while I've been driving it, have I, Bradders?" he said.

I paused.

"No," I said. "It must have happened before you drove it, Martin."

Which was strictly true. I was pretty sure the damage had been done when the dinghy had been squashed between the two houseboats on the first morning, but I was kind enough not to mention that until the Deckhand was out of earshot.

Martin didn't agree.

"The engine was just clapped out," he said, as we walked to our cars. "I'm never lucky with engines."

CHAPTER SEVENTEEN
A Prickly Point.

Berry was waiting for us when we arrived at the farm, his hand wrapped in a swathe of bandages. Apparently he'd been fishing and skewered his hand on the spikes of a catfish. He'd been in hospital for two weeks and even now his hand was sore.

"Amazing," I said. "Martin has caught hundreds of catfish in the last week and he hasn't been spiked once."

"Not hundreds," said Martin, modestly.

There followed a long discourse about what bait was best for fishing in the Richmond. Berry was a "worm" man but Big Ray, the farm labourer, was a "cheese" man. He suggested some type of local cheese which he swore never failed. All the time Martin stood there, nodding knowledgeably, and Pammie tried not to look like she was peering into Ray's mouth.

Big Fish to Rubber Ducky

Ray had a habit of taking a long blade of grass, sticking it in his mouth, chewing on it and at the same time sucking the next section into his mouth with his lips so that it, in turn, could be chewed. In this way the whole blade of grass would gradually disappear. The grass was very tough, and Ray had no teeth at all in the front of his bottom jaw. Even with her vast experience as an orthodontist, Pammie could never work out how Ray chewed the grass in the first place, or where it went after he chewed it. She would watch his mouth intently, leaning forward to get a better view as he spoke and chewed at the same time. Sometimes she was so mesmerised that she almost fell over. This time she was so intent on watching the disappearing grass that I don't think she heard Martin say he was going to buy some cheese and go fishing again after the farm inspection.

Despite his injured hand, Berry insisted on driving us around the farm as usual, in his Pajero. Given that there were nine of us, some of us had to miss out. Pammie was happy to stay in the shade near the farm shed with the baby, although I suspect she just wanted to solve the mystery of the disappearing grass; catch Ray in the act of spitting out the chewed up pith, as it were.

A Prickly Point

We had previously tied an old tractor tyre on to a tree to make a swing and after being stuck on the houseboat for a few days, Kate and Will were more than happy to stay and play on it.

So I sat beside Berry in the front, Annie and Martin sat on the rear seats, and Luc and Rohan sat in the back storage area. We could hear their shouts and groans as they bounced up and down, even before we got off the main track. Driving single-handed made this trip even more hairy than usual. Several times we went into a slide, which Berry would eventually correct, although I am not sure that we always ended up continuing in the direction he'd intended.

The idea of the drive was to travel up and down the rows of macadamia trees and hardwoods that we had planted, looking for insect infestation, storm damage, fungus or even just poor growth. To be honest, we knew so little about macadamia farming at the time, Berry could have told us anything. In fact he probably did. Who knows? But it made us feel part of the process, and occasionally we would come across a problem or decide what to do with a particular part of the farm. Mostly, we pretty much went along with Berry on detail.

This is probably why the farm is the only successful venture we have ever had together. We had nothing to do with choosing the place, and very little to do with running it.

Even so, after Berry left, we would normally walk vast areas of the farm, looking for any problems Berry or Ray had overlooked. Martin was the most zealous in this regard. He loved to catch Berry out over some "leaf gurgler" or "caterpillar infestation" he had apparently missed. Usually he'd trek to the most inaccessible parts of the farm to do this; but this time, no sooner had Berry driven off than Martin was keen to get into his car and be away.

"What's the hurry?" asked Pammie.

"I want to buy some cheese," said Martin. "I'm going fishing."

"I told you to wear a hat, Martin," Pammie said. "The sun's got to you."

Martin bought his cheese, and went fishing. His outboard wasn't fixed yet, nor was his refrigerator, so he loaded a new set of ice blocks into his freezer box on the roof of his houseboat, and took our dinghy to go fishing.

The rest of us drove down to the Ballina water slide,

to let the kids run off more energy. While Rohan and Luc raced up and down on the higher slide, Kate and Willie played on the smaller slide, and Pammie swam with the baby in the pool next door. Annie and I took it in turns to keep an eye on the older kids, and swim a few laps. Annie and Pammie decided they didn't want to cook much that night so we went to the greengrocers for fresh fruit and vegetables, got a couple of fresh baguettes from the bakery, some calamari and freshly cooked prawns and lobster from the fish market. While we were there I also picked up a whole, fresh bream.

"You know we're not cooking tonight," said Annie.

"I know," I said.

The Deckhand had fixed the Brookie's outboard by the time we got back to the marina, which was probably just as well, because despite our shouts to Martin to come and collect Pammie and the kids, he sat hunched in our dinghy on the other side of the river, back to us, studiously fishing.

I dropped Pammie and her kids onto their houseboat. Still Martin hadn't moved. I loaded Annie and the kids into the dinghy, and headed to our houseboat.

On the way, I detoured over to where Martin was fishing. As we approached, I cut the engine, and took the bream out of its wrapping.

"Caught anything?" I yelled.

"Nah," he said. "There's too many skiers and speedboats around, scaring the fish."

"Maybe they don't like cheese," I said.

"No. They like it," said Martin. "I've had some nibbles."

"Here," I said. "See if you can catch this one."

And I threw him the bream.

He wasn't ready for it, of course. Besides, he was still holding the rod. He grabbed at the fish one-handed, but it bounced off his hand, hit the side of the dinghy, and fell into the water with a splash.

"Jeez, Martin," I said. "You can't even catch a fish when it jumps into the boat."

Annie said this was childish. I pointed out that the kids thought it was funny.

"That's because they're children," said Annie. "Children laugh at childish things. That's why childish things are called childish."

Martin didn't see the funny side of it, either.

A Prickly Point

He upped anchor, and ran my dinghy back to his houseboat. As we got aboard our houseboat, Martin was already on the radio.

"Rubber Ducky to Big Fish," he said. "We're heading back up to the island where it's quieter. Over."

"This is your fault," said Annie. "We could have stayed safely moored to the buoy for the night if you hadn't teased Martin."

"Well, it's too noisy here," I said. "Too many speedboats and skiers. Martin's right. It'll be much quieter up at the island."

And it was.

The trip back to the island was the most peaceful time we spent on the houseboat. The sun was low in the sky. The water was like glass. What wind there was came from the east, behind us, so it pushed us along, rather than beat into our faces. It was no more than a breeze really, but we still moored on the far side of the island, in almost the same spots we had vacated only that morning.

We decided to have a picnic on the roof of the houseboat. The kids shelled the cooked prawns. I sliced the mangoes and chilled the white wine. Annie deep-fried the calamari, and Pammie cracked the lobsters and prepared the salad; all of which we were going to eat with fresh bread, which we hadn't had for a week.

All this time, Martin was fishing upstream. Although he now had an outboard that would start, old habits die hard, and I am sure he figured that if he did get adrift, at least he would drift past us.

The sun began to dip, and we decided to eat while there was still some light left. Pammie yelled across the water to Martin, who reluctantly upped anchor, and returned to the houseboat.

"Don't say anything," said Annie, meaning that I shouldn't mention fishing. So there was a very awkward silence as Martin came aboard. I mean, if you can't ask a fisherman if he has caught anything, what can you say to him? After a while the silence got to Martin.

"Well, go on, Bradders," he said. "Ask me."

"Ask you what?" I said.

"Ask me if I caught any fish?"

"Well, did you?"

"No."

"That's why I didn't ask," I said.

"You didn't catch any fish, either," said Pammie.

"I didn't try," I said.

"If you had, you wouldn't have caught anything," said Annie.

"Why is everybody being so aggressive?" I asked, although I knew Annie had told Pammie about the joke with the bream.

"Why don't we all enjoy the wine? And the seafood.... Even if we didn't catch it ourselves."

Rohan sniggered but Annie silenced her with a look.

The meal entered another uncomfortable silence until Luc said,

"Are we racing back to the marina, tomorrow?"

"No!" said Annie and Pammie, at the same time.
But Martin had that strange, crooked grin on his face again…

CHAPTER EIGHTEEN
Round Two...

I was awakened the following morning by the sound of Martin's houseboat engine. I wrapped a sarong around my waist, and went out on deck. To make as quiet a getaway as possible, Martin had raised the anchor on his boat before starting the engine, so that the boat was already drifting away with the current as his engine kicked in and he started to manoeuvre the houseboat around to face downstream. I could see him grinning at me through the windows of the wheelhouse.

I ran aft, switched on the fuel line to the engine; ran forward, turned on the ignition and pressed the starter button. It didn't fire. I pressed it again. It choked into life.

By this time a bleary-eyed Annie had risen from our bed and was asking what was going on?

"Bloody Martin!" I said. "He's racing us back to the marina."

"He can't race, if we don't race," said Annie, with a long-suffering look.

"No. But he'll never stop crowing about how he got there first," I said.

As if to confirm what I was saying, the radio crackled into life.

"Rubber Ducky to Big Fish. I'll wait for you at the marina. Over."

Martin had completed his turning manoeuvre, and was heading downstream to the other side of the island and the major river channel.

I opened the wheelhouse window, rushed outside, and leant through the window to put the engine into slow forward, taking the strain off the anchor so that I could winch it on board. At first the anchor refused to come loose from the river bottom.

"Shit," I said.

"I was wrong about sane and reasonable men becoming tyrants when they're put in charge of a boat," said Annie. "They simply regress to early childhood."

"Very helpful," I said, leaning back through the window, and operating the forward gear with one hand, and the winch with the other.

Eventually the anchor came loose. It wound up until it caught on the ship's rail. I couldn't reach forward to dislodge it and keep the engine going at the same time. Instead, I locked the winch off with the anchor out of the water but still hanging over the front of the boat. I ran back to the cabin to put the engine into full forward.

By now, Luc, Rohan, and Kate were also up, and standing around in the main cabin, looking sleepy and confused. I yelled at them to get out of the way.

"You should have warned us, Auntie Annie," said Rohan. "We didn't have time to hide on the roof."

The river on this side of the island is fairly narrow. It was also close to low tide now, so that much of the water was too shallow for the houseboat. It would take me ages to manoeuvre a three-point-turn and set off after Martin. By that time he would be much too far ahead to catch.

But an island is an island; I could go full steam ahead and go around the island the other way. In fact I wasn't even sure that going upstream until I reached the main branch of the river, then turning downstream with the current south of the island, wasn't actually shorter than the route Martin had taken. I did know it would be quicker than following him.

Round Two

As I reached the mainstream I headed across the river to go around a navigation buoy, which I had to keep on my left. There was no sign of Martin. I looked across to the island. Martin was steaming down the channel, which ran along the other side of the island. He was still some way ahead of me but he was on my left side; on the wrong side of the navigation buoys. To get to the main channel he would have to come out of the side channel, cross the mainstream as I'd done, and round the navigation buoys. By that time I would have reached and passed those buoys. He would be behind me.

I got onto the radio.

"Big Fish to Rubber Ducky. We'll wait for you at the marina. Over."

Martin wasn't going to give up that easily. He was still ahead of me. If he ignored the buoys, cut the corner where the channel met the mainstream, and went across to the main navigation channel at an angle, he might still beat me to it.

I watched his houseboat steer abruptly left, and head downstream near the far bank. Actually, I knew the stretch of water he was travelling on quite well.

Big Fish to Rubber Ducky

It was where I had seen the pelican standing in the water on the first day. Martin was heading over the mudflats. I got onto the radio.

"Big Fish to Rubber Ducky. There are mud flats on that side of the river. You'll get stuck. Over."

The reply came back.

"Rubber Ducky to Big Fish. We'll wait for you at the marina. Over."

Obviously he thought I was trying to trick him. He kept ploughing on.

Given the design of the houseboats, he had no vision to the side, where bemused birds stood in the shallows watching him churn past.

Nor did he have any vision of his propeller, which was throwing up a wake of brown mud across the water.

Quite soon, we had no vision of his wake either because, although his engine continued to roar, we were slowly and surely moving ahead.

The mud was slowing his progress. Then there was no progress at all.

A pall of black smoke started to billow from his engine.

I got back on to the radio.

"Big Fish to Rubber Ducky. There's smoke coming from your engine, over."

Martin didn't bother with the niceties when he replied, "Shut up, ya fool. They'll hear you in the marina."

In the background I could hear Pammie shouting,

"Switch the engine off, Martin! Switch it off! The boat's full of smoke!"

Martin's engine went dead.

"Turn around," said Annie, but I had already slowed the engine and was preparing to turn.

As I pulled alongside Martin's houseboat, making sure to stay far enough away so that we wouldn't run aground as well, Pammie, with Baby Eddie perched on one hip, was opening all the doors and windows with her free hand to let the smoke clear from the cabin. Mindful that Martin didn't want the marina to know he was in trouble, I leaned over the side of the boat and yelled,

"Do you want me to take Pammie and the kids on board, Martin?"

"There's no fire," he yelled back. "Just smoke."

"We're coming over," said Pammie.

"That's right. Abandon me," said Martin.

"A Captain has to go down with his ship, Martin,"

said Pammie. "Besides, if you hadn't been racing, we wouldn't be in this mess."

After we'd transferred Pammie and the kids to our boat by dinghy, I went across to check on the damage. The smoke had cleared by now and we could see that while the front of the houseboat bobbed on the incoming tide, the rear sat solidly on the bottom. The propeller was hidden in a mass of weed and mud and the smoke had been caused by the engine revving while the propeller was stuck fast.

"We should call the marina," I said.

"I don't want them to know," said Martin. "The tide's coming in. I can float off soon."

"Yeah. In about six hours," I said.

"Well, you tow me off," said Martin.

I had visions of us both getting stuck; so first we cut away all the mud and weed from the propeller, and then Martin threw me a line, which I took back onto our houseboat in the dinghy. I tied it to the anchor housing. I figured that had to be strong enough to hold the weight of the boat.

I put our boat into slow reverse. Gradually, Martin's houseboat inched forward, came unstuck from the mud, and floated out into the channel. The problem was, there are no brakes on a houseboat so when I stopped, by putting our engine into slow forward, Martin kept floating towards me.

I called out to him to try his engine, while I leaned over the side of the houseboat fending off his boat. He started the motor. It groaned a bit, but then seemed to take on a regular rhythm. He tried a few more revs. The engine groaned in protest. He pulled back to "Slow Ahead" again.

"I'll have to stay in low gear," He yelled.

"We'll wait for you at the marina," I called back, not being funny.

As we picked up speed, leaving Martin behind, he leaned over the rail, and yelled,

"Aren't you coming back on board, Pammie?"

"Wave goodbye to daddy," said Pammie, still holding Eddie in her arms.

The baby dutifully waved, then stared at the rest of us, wondering why we were laughing. We didn't really abandon Martin. We did move on ahead so he wouldn't bang into us, but we stayed close enough to make sure his engine didn't stop or burst into flames.

At one point, impatient with the speed, or rather the lack of it, Martin tried to increase the revs again. Again the engine groaned in protest. And again Martin had to pull back the revs, so that the houseboat just limped along.

I told Annie and the kids to pack all our bags. I didn't want to be hanging around for too long at the marina after Martin explained that he'd managed to stuff up a second engine of theirs. I had reckoned without Martin's ingenuity.

"I don't know what sort of maintenance you do on these houseboats," he told the Manager. "Our fridge hasn't worked since we got on. Your deckhand managed to pull the door off Bradder's fridge. Didn't he, Bradders?"

"Yes," I said, but Martin didn't really need my support. He went on without pausing for breath.

"First the outboard motor packed up. Now the houseboat engine is making a hell of a racket every time I put it into full forward. Do you put oil in these engines? I couldn't get any speed up. We couldn't go anywhere at that speed. Their engine was faster than ours, even when we first got on board, wasn't it, Bradders?"

Round Two

"Yes," I said.

The Manager wasn't prepared for the onslaught. All he could say was,

"We've got the new part for the fridge."

"Well it's no good now, is it?" said Martin. "We're leaving now. I reckon we ought to have a refund."

I decided to cut in before Martin went too far.

"Time we were getting on the road, Martin," I said.

But Martin was just getting warmed up. As I left the office, Martin was telling the Manager that the houseboats had serious design faults, too. You couldn't see out the back when you were in the wheelhouse. That's very dangerous. The radios only worked when you could see the other boat. What good was that? And the charts! Well the charts were just hopeless....

When I got into the car, Annie asked if Martin was going to have to pay to get the engine fixed.

"I dunno," I said. "The way things are going, I think he's more likely to be getting part of his hire fee back."

And that's exactly what happened.

CHAPTER NINETEEN
There's a Place in Tenterfield.

Annie and Pammie had changed the rules for the drive home. No short cuts over dirt roads. No meeting places during the day where we could goad each other into a race. In fact we even took different routes from Ballina to the first night's stop at Tamworth, so we wouldn't keep passing each other. Martin took the Bruxton Highway straight across the Great Dividing Range, through Tenterfield, and I travelled south, crossing the mountains on the Gwydir Highway between Grafton and Glen Innes. This was the road we'd have taken on the way up, if we hadn't taken the short cut over the dirt. Annie said she wanted to see this piece of road at least once because the views were meant to be fabulous, but the kid's were disappointed to miss Tenterfield. It had special memories for us.

We'd stopped in Tenterfield on the infamous journey

in the Tarago from Byron Bay to Sydney. There were floods at the time, so we couldn't use the Pacific Highway, which was cut both north and south of Byron. Instead, we headed inland. It is less than two hundred kilometres from Byron to Tenterfield, but because of Willie's ability to stop the Tarago at will by announcing that he wanted a "wee wee", Tenterfield was as far as we got on the first day.

Annie had found the motel after a hasty shuffle through the RACV Guide. "Heritage Listed Homestead," it said. What it omitted to say was that the owners lived in a heritage listed homestead, but the guests stayed in a concrete block which was decorated by the same Interior Designer who did the motel in Grafton. What is it with orange nylon curtains? I think somebody must have been selling them cheap in northern New South Wales about thirty years earlier. And like the Grafton motel, the pool was empty when we arrived, although in those days there was a real excuse. While the coast was in flood, Tenterfield was in the middle of a drought, and water couldn't be spared for the pool.

Annie had booked us the two-bedroom "Executive Suite." What we actually got seemed to be just one bedroom, and a sofa bed in the living room. The bedroom was dominated by a mirror surrounded by little bulbs, like the ones you see in theatre dressing rooms. The electrics were faulty and the lights kept strobing. To make matters worse, the mirror was warped. Not only did the flashing lights make you feel nauseous when you stood looking into the mirror, but your image changed shape constantly, giving you grotesque features like a swollen head or eyes that suddenly moved towards each other. The kids viewed it with some alarm until Maxie, the nanny, told them it was a special "Disco Mirror." While they entertained themselves prancing around in front of it, I went looking for the second bedroom.

When I found it, it was tiny. There was hardly room to move. It had two bunks, a single bed and a second door which I thought must be either a built-in wardrobe or hopefully, a second bathroom. I opened the door. There in front of me was a room even smaller than the one I was in, with a single bed filling most of the room. On the bed sat an ancient man, dressed only in his Y-fronts. He looked up as I opened the door.

He must have been as shocked to see me as I was to see him because his mouth dropped open and his upper set of dentures fell, so that they hung suspended in his gaping mouth.

"Sorry," I said, and closed the door.

Under certain circumstances I suffer from asthma, usually brought on by cold, damp or extreme stress. This was the only time I ever had an asthma attack brought on by hysteria. The sight of the old man had literally taken my breath away so that I was quite unable to laugh out loud. Instead, I backed into the living room gasping, and making strange, strangled noises. As I gasped for breath, so the asthma cut in, and the laughter, trapped inside, became even more hysterical. Eventually I collapsed on the sofa, still making incoherent sounds. Annie and the kids had no idea what could have brought this on. Annie was convinced I was having a heart attack and started thumping me on the chest.

"Stop! Stop!" I managed to gasp. "There's an old man in the cupboard."

I was saved from further explanation by a loud banging on the door. Maxie went to answer it. The man standing there looked and sounded like a heavyweight boxer who'd been punched once too often in the throat. How dare I burst into his father's bedroom like that, he demanded to know. I had frightened the old man half to death! I explained, as I fought to control my hysteria, that I had thought the door was a cupboard, and that we were just as surprised to find an unlocked door between him and us as he was. I suggested he should talk to the management. While he went off to "do just that" I collapsed onto the sofa, giggling helplessly again, with Annie, Maxie, and the kids staring at me in astonishment.

The lady from "the management" who came to sort out the problem was very nice, and totally useless. She explained that because of the drought, the real manager, along with most of the men in Tenterfield, had taken the local cattle on a cattle drive, grazing them along the side of the road, or indeed anywhere else they could find feed, until the rains returned. The cattlemen's wives had been left in charge of the motel and "didn't really know anything about it." They couldn't find the key to the adjoining door so would I mind jamming a chair under the doorknob, and pretending to the man next door that the door was now locked?

The same lady was behind the bar when we went up to the Heritage Listed Homestead for dinner. We ordered our drinks: scotch and ice for Annie and me, vodka and tonic for Pammie and Martin, Bacardi and coke for Maxie, and soft drinks for the kids. By now the lady must have looked on me as a friend because she took me aside to confide in me that she didn't know how to mix drinks. Normally she only did the cooking, which she had to do now. Would I mind mixing the drinks for everybody? Just help myself, and list what we drank on a piece of paper. I have to say that the drinks that night were very good.

I also have to say the food was good too; although the ambience in the Colonial Dining Room was somewhat spoilt by the fact that the Queen Anne chairs were, in fact, aluminium copies. Maybe it was the great pre-dinner drinks I'd mixed, but I failed to notice this right away. When I lifted Annie's chair to tuck it in behind her knees as she sat down, I'd expected the chair to be made of heavy mahogany, and as a result put a fair amount of effort into lifting the chair and shoving it forward. Since the chair actually weighed only about 500 grams I ended up jamming it forward with such vigour that I almost cut Annie off at the knees.

The piece de resistance of the place in Tenterfield however, was the hot water system. It was ancient, very loud, and it stood immediately outside our rooms.

It gurgled, it groaned, and it rattled as the water ran through the ancient pipes to the various bathrooms. Martin is a very light sleeper. He couldn't possibly sleep next to this noise, he said, when we returned from dinner and he went back to the Heritage Listed Homestead to complain. (I needn't tell you that the rooms had no phones.)

He came back somewhat pacified, and announced that the hot water system was on a timer and would automatically switch off in a few minutes. Sure enough, in less than a minute the gurgling, the groaning and the rattling all stopped, and we settled into an exhausted sleep, intent on an early start next morning.

What the nice lady in the Heritage Listed Homestead omitted to tell Martin was that when the hot water system went off, it stayed off for eight hours. She probably didn't know.

We awoke at first light to cold showers, and muffled conversation coming from outside the bathroom window. Eventually, Martin knocked on the door.

"Have you got any hot water?" he asked.

Of course we hadn't.

Couldn't he tell that the system wasn't working? There

was no noise coming from the water heater. It was the middle of summer, anyway. Couldn't he have a cold shower?

Given the slow progress we had made the previous day, I was keen to get on the road. Martin wouldn't budge. He couldn't face a cold shower.

Reluctantly, I went out to join the gaggle of motel guests gathered around the hot water heater. It's amazing how adversity brings people together. Included in the gathering were the heavyweight boxer and his father, both being very jolly.

"Well, I've been here twice now," joked the boxer, "The first time and the last time."

I looked at the ancient timing mechanism on the heater. It was very much a Heath Robinson affair built around what looked like an old alarm clock, with valves, dials, and pipes everywhere. As I was trying to figure out how it worked, the nice lady from the Heritage Listed Homestead came walking down the side of the Concrete Block carrying breakfast on a tray for a Bikie and his girlfriend who were occupying the suite at the very head of the row.

When she saw us she obviously anticipated trouble

because she smiled brightly, nodded, opened the serving hatch to the motel suite, pushed the tray inside, then turned and practically ran back to the safety of the Heritage Listed Homestead.

As we watched her disappear we could hear voices and banging coming from inside the Bikie's suite. Apparently access to the serving hatch on the inside of the suite was somehow blocked, and the Bikie couldn't get at his breakfast.

Suddenly, the door to the suite opened, and the Bikie's girlfriend appeared, to open the hatch from the outside and retrieve the tray.

She was a beautiful girl. She didn't look much more than sixteen, with a slim, young figure. I could tell she had a slim, young figure because she was wearing a string vest that almost came down to her waist and nothing else at all. Clearly, at this time of the morning, she hadn't expected the entire guest list of the motel to be standing outside her door, so she hadn't bothered to dress.

On first opening the door, she had looked towards the Heritage Listed Homestead to make sure the nice lady had gone and the coast was clear; but she hadn't looked in the opposite direction, before venturing out.

As she turned back from the hatch, holding the tray in one hand, keeping the room door open with the other, she came face to face with the heavyweight boxer, his father, again with his upper dentures suspended in his gaping mouth, Martin, me, and our assorted wives and children. She grabbed the tray with her second hand, and lowered it in a vain attempt to cover her nudity. Naturally this meant that the door slammed behind her, cutting off her escape.

"Keeeviin!" she yelled.

A moment later, the Bikie opened the door and she scurried inside, shrieking. The door shut behind her, then opened again. The Bikie re-emerged, glowered at the assembled group, then went back in, and slammed the door.

There was a pause, while everyone stood still staring at the Bikie's door.

"She's a very pretty girl," said Annie.

"Wish I had a figure like that," said Pammie.

I turned back to the heater.

"I don't think I can re-adjust the timing on this," I said. "Why don't we just change the time on the clock?"

Sticking my finger alongside the minute hand, I

rotated it from six-thirty to a couple of minutes past seven. The water immediately started coughing and gurgling. Almost before I'd turned around, the Brookies, the heavyweight boxer, his dad, and everyone else, including my lot, had all disappeared back into their respective suites.

Only Katie stood there.

"Why didn't that lady have any clothes on?" she asked.

Perhaps the most memorable line about the Tenterfield motel came from Martin as we sat under the verandah of the Grafton motel on New Year's Eve, watching the kids riding the spa.

We were discussing the dilapidated state of the Grafton motel and I ventured that it was the worst motel we had ever stayed in.

"No, no," said Martin, channelling the Colonel in *Fawlty Towers*. "*No, no! There's a place in Tenterfield.*"

We then had to repeat the whole story of Tenterfield to Rohan, who hadn't been there. She was very disappointed that we weren't going home via Tenterfield this time, so that she could see the famous motel with its Disco Mirror and Heritage Listed Homestead.

About half way between Grafton and Glen Innes on

the Gwydir Highway, I was beginning to regret not going that way, too. After Jackadgery, the road winds up the almost vertical face of the Gibraltar Range. It is spectacularly beautiful, with wide vistas back to the sea about fifty kilometres to the east. It is also very rugged, and totally deserted; which is why I felt a slight lump in my throat as the alarm flashed on the fuel gauge telling me that I was almost out of petrol. In my eagerness to get on the road I'd forgotten to fill the petrol tank.

I have driven through, and missed, some of the most spectacular country in Australia. Instead of having my eyes glued to the road, as I did when we descended into Nymboida on the way east over the mountains, I now had my eyes glued to the fuel gauge as we ascended back up the escarpment. It was miles since we last saw a petrol station. I decided to push on.

All the way over the mountains, past Bald Knob, and into Glen Innes, I kept a surreptitious eye on the fuel gauge. Of course I didn't tell Annie. No point in everybody in the car worrying, I reasoned. Besides, I knew she'd only tell the Brookies later.

Fortunately, we just limped into Glen Innes, where I casually suggested that we pull in and fill up the car and have some lunch at the first service station we saw.

I don't know how we made it. The fuel tank of the Integra is supposed to hold fifty litres. As the petrol gauge showed I was putting in fifty-one litres, I realised that we must have done the last few miles on the whiff of petrol fumes. I must have looked a little strange because Annie asked me if I was feeling all right.

"Yes," I said. "The drive over the mountains was a bit tiring, that's all. We should have a rest before we go on."

"That's the first sensible thing you've said on this trip," said Annie.

CHAPTER TWENTY
Round Three.

I don't know whether Martin arrived before or after us at Tamworth. We stayed at the Powerhouse Boutique Hotel. It's called a boutique hotel but by country standards it is pretty big, and we couldn't see Martin's car in the car park even though it might have been there. The first we knew that he had arrived was a call from Pammie saying they were going to the pool. Could we meet them, and make dinner arrangements?

When we got to the pool Martin was already laid out on a banana chair under an enormous umbrella, wearing his even more enormous board shorts. He was sipping a cocktail, while Pammie and the kids were swimming.

"Nice place isn't it, Bradders?" he said, looking rather glum.

"You sound disappointed," I said.

"Well, it's not as exciting as the Spa in Grafton or the Hot Water System in Tenterfield, is it?" he said.

Thus confirming my long held suspicion that Martin is only happy in the middle of the chaos, and if there isn't any, he'll create some.

Unfortunately for him, the Powerhouse Hotel seemed to be pretty well run and well located, with a Macdonald's down the road for the kids and a good in-house restaurant for the adults. There seemed little opportunity for mayhem here. The kids had been deprived of TV and fast food for over a week; they were having withdrawal symptoms, so they just wanted hamburgers, chips, and TV in the room. The adults, or more precisely Annie and Pammie, decided they would treat themselves to the first real restaurant dinner of the trip.

After a good meal, wine, and brandy with coffee, we were all feeling pretty relaxed. Obviously not a state that Martin was happy with.

"Aahve bin looking at the map," he said.

Whenever he has a few drinks, his Cornish origins start to show in his voice.

"We don't want to go through Wagga, and spend the night in Albury. If we just cut across from Ardlethan to

Round Three

Narrandera, we can cross the river at Tocumwal and be home by tomorrow night."

"I'm not taking anymore short cuts," said Annie, even though the names Martin had mentioned meant nothing to her.

They probably meant nothing to Martin either; he just hated the idea of travelling home in an orderly manner.

"Please yerself, Bradders," he said. "But Aah'll be home before you. That means Aah'll win the race."

I was feeling pretty mellow.

"I don't care," I said. "I've won every race until now. I'm happy to let you win one."

This was a red rag to a bull for Martin.

"No you 'aven't," he snapped. "I won the race to the island. You moored on the wrong side. And I would've won the race back to the marina, if my engine hadn't blown up."

"If you hadn't blown it up," I said.

"Aah well," said Martin, looking all mellow again.

"Be that as it may, the point is, it's one all. If I win round three, I *win!*"

"No you don't," I said.

"Yes I do," he said.

Annie stood up.

"I'm going to bed," she said. "Coming Ian?"

I got up.

"That's right, Bradders," said Martin "Off you go. You're going to need your sleep. You've got a long drive ahead of you in the morning."

As we drove along, early the next day, I said to Annie,

"Have you looked at the map?"

"No!" she said, and I could feel the temperature drop in the car.

I carried on, regardless.

"The road from Ardlethan to Tocumwal has got a name. It's the continuation of the Newell Highway."

Silence.

I continued.

"It can't be too bad, if it's a Highway. It's sealed all the way. And it's a lot shorter."

"I'm not driving all the way back to Melbourne in one day," said Annie.

"We don't have to," I said. "We can just drive until we get tired, then stop. There are plenty of places to stay. Tocumwal. Shepparton. Seymour. Of course, if we do get as far as Seymour, we might as well drive on home."

Round Three

"I'm not driving along the Newell Highway," said Annie.

"Well, actually," I said, "We're driving along it now."

The chill in the car lifted after about an hour. Not just because there was no point Annie getting upset about something which had already happened, and not just because the road was pretty good anyway; more because, ahead of us, we noticed what looked like a dust storm.

It's amazing how out of touch you can get, spending a week on a houseboat. We hadn't watched TV, listened to the radio or even read a newspaper. We didn't know that half of southern New South Wales was ablaze with bushfires.

We didn't know the Newell Highway was cut between Finley and Tocumwal. How could we? How could Martin? I'm sure it was just bad luck that he suggested we travel this route.

To get from New South Wales to Victoria, you have to cross the Murray River somewhere, so we had two choices. We could travel west to Deniliquin, and cross the river at Echuca, or we could travel east, and cross the river at Albury.

At least, I thought we had two choices.

I had forgotten that all of the other occupants of the car were Lucases or descendants of Lucases.

In case you're confused, that means Annie's side of the family, after whom our son is named.

The thing about Lucases is that, when it comes to real danger, they have no more regard for their personal safety than Martin does. That's why they all love riding on Corkscrews and Lethal Weapons at Amusement Parks while I stay safely on the ground.

That's why, when I turned left at Finlay and headed towards Albury and away from the fire, they all yelled as we passed through Berrigan that there was a sign showing Cobram and Tocumwal to our right, and maybe *that* road was open. Maybe we could skirt the fire and still cross the river at Tocumwal. Reluctantly, I agreed to try. It felt like the first, and last time, they coerced me onto the Big Dipper. I was in a cold sweat, and the kids and Annie were bubbling with excitement.

They get this recklessness from Annie's father, Maurice, who was part Burmese. Annie always claimed that her grandmother was a Shan, a mountain tribeswoman, and that the Shan were head-hunters. I am prepared to believe this.

Round Three

During the war Maurice, and his wife, Rose, were interned by the Japanese in Malaya. Being Eurasian, they were considered hostile neutrals. They weren't kept in the POW camps with the Allied forces. Instead, the Japanese transported them, along with 1500 others, to the jungle-covered west coast of the peninsular. They were given food and seed sufficient for three months, and told that henceforth they must fend for themselves. Most of the internees were urban dwellers, clerks or teachers like Maurice and Rose. They knew nothing about farming, and they were convinced that before the three months were up, the British would return to rescue them. So they ate the food. They cooked, and ate the grain. They sat around, and waited for their rescuers to appear. Unfortunately, the British didn't return for three years.

Maurice was one of the few internees who didn't rely on the British. He took Rose deep into the jungle where he built a hut, hidden from all but the most dedicated of searchers. He planted the seed, again concealing the plantation in the jungle. He learnt from the local Malays how make fish traps in the streams, and hunted with the Chinese Communist guerrillas, who were also hiding in there.

Big Fish to Rubber Ducky

When the three months had passed, people began to starve. Maurice had to protect his crops from his own compatriots. He had barely enough to support himself and Rose; nothing to share. During their time in the jungle, Rose caught Blackwater fever, a complication of malaria, and had two miscarriages largely because of poor diet and contaminated water. Of the fifteen hundred Eurasians interned with them, less than three hundred survived the war.

Maurice and Rose survived because they were hidden so deeply in the jungle that when the war ended, they didn't even know about it for three months. Eventually the British, in need of teachers and other professionals to help the traumatised country get back on its feet, had to send scouts into the jungle to find Maurice, and persuade him to leave his hiding -place, and return to his former life as a school headmaster. It brought to an end what must have been an horrific time in their lives.

Forty-five years later, in Perth, I sat down with Maurice and recorded his story with a view to one-day making it into a film. As I sat opposite him, recalling his adventures all those years ago, I was amazed to find that he actually spoke of events with affection.

Round Three

At the end of the interview, so that I could get the essence of the story, I asked him if he could describe in a sentence his overall impression of the war?

Maurice's eye's lit up. Like many Eurasians, he had difficulty pronouncing the "th" sound.

"It was t'rilling," he said. "Absolutely t'rilling. They had to drag me out of the jungle at the end of the war. I never wanted to leave."

That was the attitude I was surrounded by in the car. As we drove south from Berrigan to Barooga, we could see the flames in the bushland to our right. Even though the fire was some way off, I could feel its heat in the car.

"Isn't it 'citing?" said Kate.

"T'rilling," I said. But I didn't mean it.

In Barooga, the road back to Tocumwal was apparently still open but I could see outbreaks of fire on both sides of the road. They were just small scrub fires, but I wasn't prepared to drive past them. If the road was closed further down and I had to turn back, the scrub fires could have turned into raging infernos.

I decided not to risk it; to turn left, and head along the river valley instead.

"The road's not closed," said Lucas. "There are no signs up."

But I was determined.

"Martin'll get home before us," said Lucas.

"I'm turning back," I said firmly. "I didn't want to come this way in the first place."

"Well, I didn't want to take a short cut in the first place," said Annie, as if all this was my fault.

The kids fell into a gloomy silence. Where was the fun in driving safely along one of the most beautiful river valleys in Australia, when you could be risking your life driving through bush fires?

"I wonder if Pammie and Martin are all right," said Annie. "They'd have been ahead of us"

"I bet *they* got through," said Luc, in a way that suggested that I was no longer his greatest hero.

CHAPTER TWENTY-ONE
Lemmings and Big Fish.

Convinced now that Martin would get back to Melbourne first, I found the trip suddenly took on a more relaxed atmosphere. We drove along to Corowa, crossed the river, and booked into a motel in Rutherglen. After the heat of the drive and the bushfires, the swimming pool and spa were very inviting.

"This is nice," said Annie, as she soaked in the spa. "Why wasn't the whole holiday like this? Why is it we're always racing around when we go on holiday with the Brookies?"

I shrugged.

"Just something in Martin's nature, I suppose," I said.

Annie said nothing, but I could tell what she was thinking from the way she looked at me.

"It's in Man's nature to be competitive," I said, "When you're at work, there's plenty of competition. It's good to come home and relax. When you're on holiday......"

"You spend the whole time racing houseboats, cars, and anything else you can find," Annie finished the sentence for me. "That makes a lot of sense."

The insincerity of her conclusion was palpable but I decided to ignore it, gracefully.

"Well," she continued "The Brookies are home by now. There's nobody to race. You don't have to be back at work for a couple of days. We'll have a nice leisurely drive home. There are a few good vineyards around here. I'd like to visit a couple tomorrow."

I have to admit the next day was pleasant. We got up late. The kids had a swim before breakfast. We visited a couple of vineyards, and although I had to be a bit circumspect with the tasting, we bought some good wines to take home with us.

It was late afternoon when we eventually drove down to Wangaratta and headed for the Hume Highway which would take us on the last leg towards Melbourne.

As we drove past a garage in Wangaratta, Lucas called out,

"There's Martin's car!"

I didn't think it was. It couldn't be, I said, but Annie

pointed out that there aren't too many Renaults of that vintage and colour driving around country Victoria. Maybe they'd had an accident? We should turn back and check.

As we drove into the garage, we could see that it was indeed Martin's car, although it didn't look like it had been in any accident.

Martin was rummaging around in the boot. I got out of our car and walked over to him.

"What happened to the car?" I asked.

He jumped, startled, turned to see who had snuck up behind him, and gave me that crooked grin.

"Bradders!" he said. "I thought you'd be home in Melbourne by now."

"We got held up by the bushfires," I said.

"So did we," said Martin. "We had to detour, but we still would have got to Melbourne yesterday if the engine hadn't seized up."

I stared at him in admiration.

"That's three engines you've blown up, on one trip." .

"I know," he said. "I've never had much luck with engines."

Spare parts for Renaults aren't exactly commonplace

in country Victoria, so Martin and Pammie had been forced to book into a motel while they waited for the spare part to be shipped up. It was due to arrive that morning, and once the Renault was fixed, they'd be heading for home again, he said. In the meantime, Pammie and the kids were relaxing by the motel pool, and he had gone fishing. He'd only returned to the car to collect the esky.

"Taking some tinnies down to the river?" I asked.

"No," he said, "I've got to keep the fish cold."

"You're a bit optimistic, aren't you?" I said.

He grinned, and opened the esky to reveal several good-sized fish.

"I caught 'em in the local river," he said, proudly. "You know what bait I used?"

I shrugged.

"Worms? Flies?"

"No," he said. "Old Ray's cheese. It's great. When we get back to Melbourne, you must come over to dinner. We'll cook the fish."

I asked him if Pammie and the kids were all right? Asked if there was anything I could do? But he seemed quite content, so I decided we'd drive on to Melbourne.

Lemmings and Big Fish

As I turned to get back into the car, he called out,

"Hey, Bradders? Great holiday. We should hire those houseboats again next year."

"Yes," I said.

"Lemmings," I thought, and got into the car.

Annie asked if everybody was alright.

"Sure," I said. "Martin's just blown another engine. Nothing unusual."

As we drove on, Katie asked,

"Where's Willie and Baby Eddie?"

"They're staying in a motel until the garage fixes their car," I said.

"So they haven't been home to Melbourne, yet?" asked Lucas, in an offhand way.

"No," I said, looking at him in the rear view mirror, and grinning.

Katie clapped her hands.

"We won!" she said.

The older kids laughed, but Annie wasn't amused.

"Now look what you've done," she said.

"What?" I said.

"You've got Katie doing it now. She was the only sane one left in the family."

"Hold on," I said. "None of this was my fault!

"It was your idea in the first place, the whole thing." Annie said.

I shook my head.

"I just happened to mention that we'd had some good times on a houseboat on the Myall Lakes. No sane, normal couple, with two kids under the age of three, could possibly take that as an invitation to drive four thousand kilometres to spend a week on a flood-swollen river in a three-tonne steel barge, now could they?"

THE END

POSTSCRIPT

Against all odds, the macadamia farm thrived and the Bradleys and Brooks each developed successful businesses based on its produce.

The Brooks established Brookfarm, specializing in macadamia muesli, nuts and oils. Brookfarm is now one of the biggest employers in Byron Bay.

The Bradleys created their Australian Bush Christmas Cakes, which are sent all over the world today. They are dark fruit cakes made to a recipe inspired by the indigenous fruit and flavours of the Northern Rivers region including, of course, macadamia nuts.

And while Martin and Ian have ably assisted their wives, they have to admit that these enterprises have gone so smoothly because, this time, the women were at the helm.

*****

Big Fish to Rubber Ducky is also available in ebook form from Amazon, iBooks, Smashwords and other retailers.

THE OSMIUM MARBLES

They destroyed their own planet.
Now they want to *save* ours?

A NEW ECO-SCI-FI NOVEL FROM THE AUTHOR OF "BIG FISH TO RUBBER DUCKY."

Publishing October 23, 2015
PRE-ORDER NOW
at the discounted price of
$2.99
From Smashwords
https://www.smashwords.com/books/view/552774
Formatted for Kindle, iBook and most other devices.

At any given moment, there are over half a million pieces of space junk in orbit around the world. NASA says manmade space debris has been dropping out of the sky at an average rate of one object a day for the past 50 years. Most controlled re-entries are set for a splashdown in the southern Pacific Ocean. If they hit land, it is usually Australia. But not all of the stuff falling out of the sky *is* manmade. When a group of tourists souvenir eight osmium marbles from a crash site in Outback Australia, they set off a chain of events that will change the world.

THE PARTHIAN SHOT

They are planning the perfect crime.
They only have two problems: they hate each other and…they are already in prison.

A NEW NOVEL FROM THE ORIGINAL
PRODUCER AND CO-WRITER OF
"PRISONER CELL BLOCK H"

Publishing March 27, 2016
PRE-ORDER NOW
at the discounted price of
$2.99
From Smashwords

https://www.smashwords.com/books/view/553162
Formatted for Kindle, iBook and most other devices.

An inquiry into the death of a female inmate in a privately run Australian prison recently uncovered lax security, corruption, and sexual misconduct.

- Staff members engaged in illicit sex while on night duty.

- Women on Day Release, working in a local brothel.

- Drugs and alcohol habitually thrown in over the fence.

In a word, *chaos*.

The perfect cover for the perfect crime.

ABOUT THE AUTHOR

Ian Bradley was born in Bath, England. He emigrated to Australia in 1965 while still technically a minor, and spent the next ten years supporting himself as a professional gambler.

In 1975 he switched to writing and producing for television. His first production *Prisoner; Cell Block H*, was a success not only in Australia but also in the USA, and the UK. This was followed by a string of critical, and commercial successes, including the award-winning dramas *The Great Bookie Robbery*, and *Embassy*.

He was Head of Production for Kerry Packer, CEO of Crawford Productions, and Vice President of Drama for Grundy Worldwide.

Ian lives in Sydney. He is the husband of actress, writer, and cake-maker, Anne Lucas; father of screenwriter, Kate Bradley and video producer/director, Lucas Bradley; and grandfather of Charlotte Rose Bradley (aged 11months) He spends his time writing, travelling, and playing golf.

***

You can contact Ian on: bigfish2rubberducky@gmail.com

www.ingramcontent.com/pod-product-compliance
Lightning Source LLC
Chambersburg PA
CBHW031349040426
42444CB00005B/236